**Praise for Pink Politics**

"Never have we needed more women in public office to bring new ideas, energy and values. Now any woman who wants to run has a book with easy-to-follow recipes for cooking up a winning campaign. Good job, Kathy Groob."
*Marie Wilson*
*Founder and President Emeritus of The White House Project*

. . . . .

"Kathy hits the mark when it comes to telling her story and giving pointers all at the same time. It will make you shake your head, nod, laugh and cry all at the same time—probably because of our kinship as women. This is not only for women, it's also for you secure men like our husbands, so get your highlighters ready, you will need a few of them."
*Debbie Halvorson*
*Former Congresswoman and Illinois Senate Majority Leader*

. . . . .

"Impressive. A 'must read' for any women candidate. Step-by-step primer on how to build a winning campaign, built on the wisdom of scores of races–assembled together to benefit all women seeking elected office. Research shows women hesitate to run because they don't feel qualified–this book gives them the practical 'nuts and bolts' information needed to overcome those concerns, run and WIN!"
*Siobhán "Sam" Bennett*
*President/CEO Women's Campaign Fund*

"You'd be hard pressed to find a stronger champion for women than Kathy Groob. Women need to read this book and run!"
*Vicki Prichard*
*Political consultant and Emmy-award winning writer*

.....

"Pink Politics offers women a comprehensive, practical guide to running for office. Women need and want details about the challenges they will face before they throw their hats in the ring. Kathy Groob is helping women identify those issues, while allowing them to see that they can run for office and win."
*Mayor Diane Whalen*

# PINK
# POLITICS

## The Woman's Practical Guide
## To Winning Elections

# Kathy Groob

Political consultant and founder

 ElectWomen

*November Strategies Publishing*

First Edition
ISBN: 978-0615549705

Quantity Purchases
Organizations, groups, clubs and other organizations may qualify for special terms when ordering quantities of this book. For information email sales@novemberstrategies.com.

November Strategies Publishing
www.NovemberStrategies.com

# Table of Contents

## PART III   SECRETS TO WINNING

## PART IV     RESOURCES FOR WOMEN CANDIDATES

# Acknowledgements

This book is dedicated to the two most important women in my life, my mother Joan Shockey and my daughter Meghan Groob. My mother's generation did not have the choice or the ability to participate as candidates except in a very limited way. My daughter's generation is the future for women in politics and with encouragement and mentoring, today's young women will engage politically and will change the face of politics in America forever.

A special thanks to Sam Bennett, Jennifer Brunner, Angie Cain, Sue Cassidy, Gale Cherry, Denise Harper Angel, Doug Heyl, Teresa Isaac, Chris Jahnke, Kathleen Lape, Jennifer Lawless, Kim McMillan, Jill Miller-Zimon, Linda Newell, Ayanna Pressley, Vicki Prichard, Rick Svatora, Julie Smith-Morrow, Brandon Thorn, Susan Westrom, Marie Wilson, and Loren VanDyke Wolff.

Thank you as well to my great friends and family: Mary Bell, Patty Burns, Emily Droege, Becky Haake, Joyce Hubbell, Barb Jasper, Virginia Johnson, Karen Landwehr, Wyona King, Tai Schulte,

Gina Smith, Patty Suedkamp, Barb Thoss, Judy White, Barb Wells, and Aimee Wulfeck.

Finally, a special thank you to my husband Jeff Groob for all his encouragement when I ran for office and for encouraging me to put my passion to work for women candidates.

# Introduction

Women are under-represented inside the political decision-making powerhouse in the United States. Despite being 53% of the voters, women hold only 17% of the seats in Congress. Within the 50 states there is even greater disparity. Of the 50 governors in America, just six are women, and 23 states have never had a female governor. Eighteen states currently have no women representing them in Congress. Three states—Vermont, Iowa and Mississippi—have never had a female representative or senator in Congress.

These statistics keep me awake at night and they should keep us all focused on one goal: to bring more women into the political process.

Women are running for public office, but not in great enough numbers to break the cycle of male dominance. Women under 40 are nearly absent from holding political office, yet they are the very voices needed to help shape policy and offer the perspective of working professionals, mothers, caretakers and community activists.

"Until we have more women in elected office, we are denying ourselves our greatest American potential," says Madeleine Kunin, first woman governor of Vermont.

In 1940, Eleanor Roosevelt said "people thought that women were going to revolutionize the conduct of government, yet all we were given was the right to vote." In 2011 we are still waiting for women to make their impact upon our government at all levels.

Researchers and universities have taken up the cause to find out what keeps women from running. The Center for American Women and Politics provides a wealth of data on tracking women who run for public office, and offers campaign training and initiatives to engage more women in the process.

Jennifer Lawless, Director of American University's Women & Politics Institute, is a leader on politics and gender studies and is the author of *It Still Takes a Candidate: Why Women Don't Run for Office*. In her 2008 report on why women are less likely to run for office than men, Lawless cites a number of factors. "Women are less likely than men to be willing to endure the rigors of a political campaign. They are less likely than men to be recruited to run for office. They are less likely than men to have the freedom to reconcile work and family obligations with a political career. They are less likely than men to think they are qualified to run for office, and they are less likely than men to perceive a fair political environment."

"Women perceive the electoral environment to be biased against women and so their rational response is 'I'm not going to run,'" adds Lawless.

"It is still political recruitment and self-perceived qualifications that are holding women back," says Lawless. Her book *It Still Takes a Candidate* details the data from the research and interviews of 3,800 women in the likely candidate categories.

While these are the perceived risks and obstacles for many women to step up and run for office, when they do run, women can be strong, effective candidates. Women can and do win.

In 2009, New Hampshire made headlines with the first state legislative chamber to have a majority of women members. The women made a significant positive impact on public policy including public funding for kindergarten.

Female legislators are more likely to fight for traditional women's and family issues relating to education, children and healthcare, and they are more likely to respect other's viewpoints and compromise when necessary to move the legislative process forward. "Women have been documented as having more collaborative, communicative leadership styles," says Katie Fischer Ziegler, Policy Specialist at the Women's Legislative Network of National Conference of State Legislators.

While training programs for female candidates are not available in every state, the movement is growing and the focus on recruitment and training is in line with what the research shows is needed for women to enter the political arena.

South Carolina is ranked as the worst state in the country for women serving in state legislatures, but they did elect their first woman governor in 2010, Republican Nikki Haley. The Southeastern Institute for Women in Politics is a bipartisan organization of women dedicated to recruiting and training women to run for public office. Based in South Carolina, the organization connects with women from across the state to narrow the gender gap and develop female political leaders.

Emerge America is a national organization operating in nine states to recruit and train Democratic women for public office. The organization's mission is to provide extensive and comprehensive training for future female candidates and to fill their training classes with at least 40% women of color.

When I founded ElectWomen in late 2008, my goal was to provide inspiration and the resources that women need when considering a bid for office. Insights not from men, but directly from other women; women who have been in the trenches, running for and working in campaigns for elected office.

I'm a big believer that the more we see women running for office—on television, in newspapers and on internet sites—the more women will run. For so long, it was predominately white men in suits on Sunday morning political talk shows, on nightly news, in print and on the internet. ElectWomen features women running for office at all levels, from school boards to U.S. Senate and beyond. I even featured a story about an extraordinary young woman running for her high school junior class presidency. After following her campaign, we were pleased to break the news that she had won her election.

*Pink Politics* is for women running for office and for those who support them. It offers the insights, best practices and secrets nobody talks about, along with war stories that other women have shared in their quest to become elected. Their stories and experiences will inspire and equip women to go the distance and win. I hope you enjoy the journey. I know I have and wouldn't take a moment of it back.

Here's my story.

# Part I

## A Life-Changing Decision

*"Even if I have to stand alone, I will not be
afraid to stand alone. I'm going to fight for you.
I'm going to fight for what's right. I'm going to
fight to hold people accountable."*
*Senator Barbara Boxer*

Making the decision to run for public office is not something to take
lightly. It will change your life. Being a candidates thrusts you into
the public spotlight. Everything in your life and in your past is fair
game for the electorate. Although you will become the candidate, you
will not run alone. You will need people to help you, and will need to
make a personal sacrifice that is similar to becoming a professional
athlete.

*Pink Politics*

# 1

# My Story

*"When I ran for office it changed my life."*
*Kathy Groob*

My political life began like so many other women who enter the political arena. It began when someone said to me, "You should run for office." Even though I had been a high school student council president, it never occurred to me to think about a run for public office. I was too busy being a businesswoman, wife and mother.

I was a political novice when I set out on my first campaign for city council. I did some of the little things wrong, but I did the big things right. From campaign finance violations to knocking on doors without a list, my first experience felt like I was fumbling through a circus maze. What I had going for me was that I was a well-known community activist and had a background in marketing that really came in handy.

My decision to run was borne out of a frustration with our current city council and a mayor who wasn't listening. I was elected on my first try out of a field of 15 candidates, almost finishing first in a race for just eight seats on the non-partisan council. When I left city council four years later, I was proud of my accomplishments and had made a real difference for our community.

The next phase of my political career began when the local party chair asked me to run against a long-serving, extremely conservative state senator. This race was a partisan seat that would require going up against an opponent who was serving in the majority party at a time when the tides were shifting away from a once-entrenched Democratic Party that had held power in my state for decades.

I took seven months to make the decision. During those seven months, I made the rounds talking to influential men in my region and whatever women I could find, and then finally launching my campaign. Working with a local political consultant, I gave the incumbent a serious challenge by raising a lot of money and running a professional campaign. But the timing was wrong, and despite my best effort, I lost by six percentage points.

The day after the election I went back to work, to my regular life, and put the whole thing behind me, vowing never to run for office again.

Four years later, I could hear my mother's voice inside my head saying, "Never say never".

When the governor of my state asked me to run for the senate seat again I could not say no. And deep down I knew the political landscape was better, and that this could be my time. I didn't want to wake up some day at 70 years old knowing I had another chance and didn't take it.

This time I knew what I was getting into and what it would take to win. I gained the necessary resource commitments and was able to work with some of the nation's top campaign strategists and pollsters. I quit my job and left my career in order to devote all my time and energy to the campaign, and worked non-stop for months raising money and knocking on doors. All signs pointed to a close race but a possible victory. We had the momentum heading into Election Day.

It was 6:30 a.m. on Election Day when the phone rang. I was looking forward to sleeping in a little, watching the morning shows in bed, and taking my time getting ready that morning. The early phone call woke us and my husband Jeff took the call from a frantic friend who was saying "I voted for Kathy but I'm not sure it registered, the button didn't light up."

That was just the first of several calls we received during the next hour and a half. Every call was reporting the same problem—when voting straight ticket, all the buttons lit up except in my race for Senate District 23.

By 9:30 a.m. our lawyers were in court and the judge ordered that all the machines causing the particular problem (a new model of handicapped-accessible machines) be locked and no one else permitted to cast a vote on them.

Most polling locations within the 73 precincts in my senate district had just two machines, one of the old traditional voting machines and one new electronic, handicapped-accessible machine. This was 2008, the year of Barack Obama. Record turnouts were expected. Lines of voters were backing up early.

Prepared for anything, expecting negative attacks and smears, I expected every dirty trick except for one—cheating on Election Day. Our county board of elections was under the control of a newly-elected clerk that had just replaced a long-time, well-respected clerk that had not run for re-election the year before. The new clerk was of the opposite party and lacked the experience needed to run a high-turnout presidential election.

The balance of power in the senate hung upon the outcome of just a couple of senate races. My race was considered the most competitive race in Kentucky that November.

In 2008, counties in Kentucky were required to use new machines for the first time that were more accessible for handicapped individuals. Each voting precinct had at least one new handicapped-accessible machine and at least one of the traditional machines. State law requires that all machines be tested right before Election Day. As voters lined up beginning at 6 a.m., people were using both types of machines in order to move quickly through the voting lines.

Unfortunately, a consistent malfunction occurred when a voter pushed the straight-ticket button for either party. Every race lit up except for one—the senate race between me and my opponent. The court ordered an immediate shut-down of all the new handicapped machines that morning, but the new county clerk had no mechanism in place to communicate that decision to all the precincts in my district. We learned throughout that day the new machines were in fact still being used. One report came in as late as 4:30 p.m.—just an hour and a half before the polls closed—that the new machines were still being used in some precincts.

Attorneys and State Party officials descended upon my county and were on the scene at the county clerk's office until 11 p.m. on election night. We left our campaign victory party, with more than 150 people still waiting for results, not knowing the outcome, only that we were due in court the next morning.

The county clerk and attorney summoned the manufacturer and programmer of the new machines, who testified that there had been a programming error in the way the machines were programmed. They said it was an accident that was not caught by the clerk because he failed to check to see that the machines were working properly. New machines were installed in county voting precincts in the 120 counties throughout Kentucky and in hundreds of races on Election

Day. My race was the only one with a "clerical" error, and we were the only systemic malfunction reported that day. We weren't buying it.

The judge ordered that a hand count of the tapes from the new machines be conducted, and that both parties should come together to supervise the counting and interpretation of voter intent on those ballots that were not clear.

Attorneys on both sides participated in the two-day tallying and recounting. The outcome showed that I trailed by 800 votes, less than a 0.5% margin. One of the attorneys on our team described the process as tedious and said in many cases "you really can't tell what the voter intended—the results just didn't make sense."

The election debacle dragged on for two weeks. It became evident that the outcome wasn't going to change. Officially, I lost by about 800 votes—one-half of a percentage point—and conceded the election. Further legal challenge didn't make much sense because the challenge would go before the elected body for which I was running— the Kentucky Senate—which was controlled by my opponent's party and a senate president who was not known for his ability to be fair.

I was devastated. I knew there was a possibility of losing when I entered the race, but I wanted to win or lose fair and square. All those months, all that hard work, and when all was said and done, I felt cheated. I wasn't sure I could get over this.

But I did survive, and I learned that *from defeat comes strength*. I soon realized after lots of tears and a feeling of depression that I had not failed. It was not my failure. I ran the best campaign I possibly could, had all the resources I needed, had so many wonderful people helping me and cheering me on, and that at the end of the day, I still had my family, friends and many good years ahead. I took a little time off to re-focus, pick up the pieces and start over.

Since I had quit my job to run, I had to get busy again and quick. My husband was there for me and offered great support and ideas as well. He suggested that I search down deep for what I was truly passionate about and spend my time focused on that.

Having been a long-time advocate for women in the work-place, a strong women's rights feminist, and a pro-woman candidate supporter, my passion was obvious. I was most passionate about seeing more women elected in my lifetime and most of all, a women president of the United States.

I channeled that passion into founding *ElectWomen*, speaking engagements, training and advocacy for women candidates and political consulting. I'm doing the work I love and in my heart, I believe I'm making a difference. I only hope that I can make a difference for you.

# 2

# Friends and Family

*"To us, family means putting your arms
around each other and being there."*
*Barbara Bush*

R unning for public office is a life-changing decision. It is a
very positive experience for most people, and the success of
the candidate and ultimately of the elected official depend greatly
upon support from their family. It is important to know that everything that impacts the candidate, especially the adjustment in their
personal life schedule, also impacts her spouse and other family
members.

As a woman, you've probably spent a great deal of your life taking care of others and providing care for your children, parents, brothers and sisters, friends, co-workers as well as volunteering your time to help others. Women are the nurturers in our society and excel at giving help, support and their time.

One of the first steps in running for office as a woman is to ask for all those people to whom you've given so much to give back to you. Without strong support from family, friends and community it is nearly impossible for today's busy women to run for political office at any level.

There is no such thing as one size fits all when it comes to the families of female candidates. Some candidates are married and can count on a spouse to fill in around the house and pick up the bulk of the domestic chores during the campaign season. Other candidates are single and count on a sister, mother, children or friends to help support their needs while campaigning.

Bottom line—there is no one like family and close friends, and unless you ask them for help, they might not otherwise understand what is needed to run an effective political campaign. Ask your closest family and friends for help and be specific about what you need.

**Sample family questions**

- Will you volunteer to put up yard signs?
- Will you drive and go with me to important candidate events?
- Will you work the greeting and money tables at events?
- Will you walk with me on Saturdays during the fall?
- Can you pick up my kids from soccer so I can knock on doors?

Ask your family and closest friends to keep your candidacy confidential until you give them the green light to begin telling people.

When I ran for city council, it was in a small city of 8,500 residents with just seven precincts. I was able to do most of the work myself, but it was our son Jason who helped spread the word at our neighborhood high school, engaging his friends to wear t-shirts and get 18-year-olds and teachers to vote for me. My husband Jeff and I put up all the campaign signs and I did door-to-door voter contact by myself.

Running for a state legislative seat is another story. It was going to take several hundred thousand dollars to win 73 precincts. I knew I needed help and that my organizational skills would come in handy when it came to gathering people together and delegating tasks and responsibilities.

Once my decision was made, I held a family meeting with my four brothers and my mom to tell them about my plans to run for the Kentucky senate. I felt it was important that they understand that sometimes family members are brought into the spotlight, especially in today's online world with bloggers and Facebook.

My brothers, their spouses and children turned out to be great supporters and campaigners. My young nieces had great fun participating in parades and events. My aunt and cousins were faithful supporters and I could always count on them for help. My mom was my best campaigner and was terrific making phone calls to strangers asking them to vote for me. My campaigns were big family affairs and I couldn't have done it without them.

My family members hosted events, participated in parades, distributed campaign literature and bumper stickers to friends and neighbors, and provided support at fundraisers. My mother made calls to senior citizens asking "will you vote for my daughter?" It was very effective.

The big surprise for many new candidates is that there is not always a strong political party organization that will provide enough volunteers for all of your campaign needs. It is critical that you solicit volunteers from within your circles: family, friends, co-workers, church and synagogue members, boards and organization members, neighbors, high school buddies, your children's parents and your vendors.

Yes, that's right, your vendors. All the people you've been paying for years for services—hairdresser, insurance agent, home repair vendors and so on. You will be surprised how many of them will help you either with their time or by making a financial contribution.

## Volunteer Circles

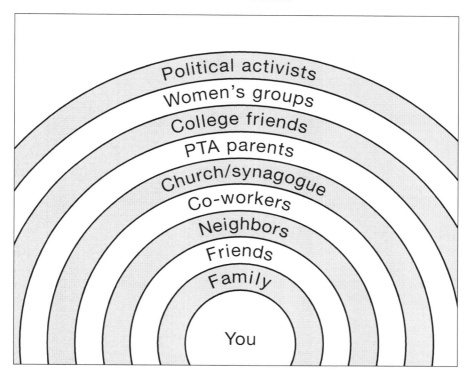

Most folks are never given the opportunity to engage in a political campaign from the inside. If you ask for help, people will give it. The more goodwill you've put out in the world, the more help you will receive when you really need it. Just remember: ask for *specific* help.

A women's grassroots organization called The Pittsfield Massachusetts WHEN group wanted to change the direction of their city government by electing women to its city council. Recruiting women candidates was difficult as they listened to potential women candidates list their barriers to running for public office. A combination of job issues, children, family obligations and money were just some of those obstacles. The WHEN group mobilized women volunteers and provided solutions to every challenge.

"We provided child care, child transportation, meal preparation along with campaign coaching," says board member Ann Pasko. "We groomed the candidates for speeches and public appearances along with taking care of their personal needs so they could campaign around the clock."

Colorado state senator Linda Newell's daughters were the ones that encouraged her to enter a tough race in 2008. Knowing her chance at winning the district was a long shot, it was her daughters that made the difference by telling her "Mom, you absolutely have to do this."

Jennifer Lawless, Director of American University's Women & Politics Institute and author, says research shows that family roles are "not making an impact upon a female candidate's decision to run, although marital and family circumstances can make those decisions more complex."

Organizing friends and family into committees is a great way to engage everyone in a meaningful way and to make sure all the critical campaign components are covered. Even in high-level congressional races, volunteers are needed to head up committees.

### Campaign Committees Needing Volunteer Chairs

| | |
|---|---|
| Advisory | Phone banking |
| Field operations | Precincts |
| Finance | Volunteers |
| Netroots (internet grassroots) | Yard signs |
| Parades | Young professionals |

Committee chairs should be well-trusted friends and family that you know will stick with you through months of hard work. Keeping everyone involved and engaged is a challenge, and good committee chairs will stay in regular touch with their committee members.

**The Candidate's Spouse**

How your spouse handles your campaign for office can be the difference in being a confident, successful candidate and one who is hanging on by a thread.

When I ran for office, my husband would jokingly refer to himself as "Mr. Kathy." He laughed it off, but I was cognizant of how invisible he felt at times. Always in the background and always standing by supportive in his role as the candidate's spouse. Especially for women candidates, the spouse role can be a tricky one to define.

A husband can't appear too controlling or domineering or it makes the woman candidate seem like she can't do it alone. He can't appear too wimpy or quiet or it will seem like she "wears the pants" in the family. Some male spouses take on the role of business manager, taking care of financial matters, organizing and putting up signs and participating in strategy meetings.

Female spouses typically support their husbands as candidates by taking care of details for events, making phone calls, writing postcards, baking cakes and keeping the household and family going while the husband campaigns.

Chris Jahnke, Washington D.C. media and speech coach, says the higher-level races become even dicier for husbands of female candidates: "It can be tricky particularly when women are running for chief executive positions like governor or President. There was a great deal of speculation about what Bill would be called if Hillary were elected President. Would he be the First Man or what?"

Spouses are often involved as chief fundraiser in lower dollar campaigns. Depending on their own personal networks, spouses can also help broaden the circle of potential donors.

Angie Cain, a political consultant with November Strategies, describes the role of the female candidate's spouse in this way: "He should simply continue to play his role as a spouse. The spouse should not become involved in managing the campaign or the candidate... that should be left up to the professionals hired to run the race. Spouses should, of course, be very supportive and be the candidate's most loyal volunteer. That means taking very active roles in the campaign such as attending events, making phone calls, knocking on doors and putting up yard signs (not to mention being helpful in the home while the candidate is out on the campaign trail). Spouses should be prepared and willing to accept the fact that their family life will be much different for several months during the campaign. Both spouses must fully commit to sacrifice a lot of time and effort in order to be successful on Election Day."

As a mother of two boys, Judge Kathleen Lape could not have run for re-election without the support of her husband. "My husband Mike is a physician with a demanding schedule but spent every free moment of his time on the campaign trail and taking care of our two boys. He put up signs, drove the truck in parades, managed the kids during parades, took care of scraped knees, and he promoted me endlessly to anyone who would listen—staff, colleagues, patients and total strangers. So many people told me they would see Mike putting up signs, even in a driving rain, while dressed in his scrubs, late at night—he did whatever it took to put up campaign signs."

"On the home front, my husband took up the slack for me," recounted Judge Lape. "He made sure homework was completed, teeth were brushed, lunches were packed and that uniforms were clean. Mike also took very good of the candidate—me. He made sure I took vitamins, remained healthy, ate breakfast every morning and got enough sleep (when I could). Each morning he would pack a cooler with water and snacks so that I could be out knocking on doors right after court finished each afternoon. He packed that cooler every day for four months!"

Although the role of the candidate spouse varies from race to race, the reality is that the campaign is about the candidate, and spouses at many times can feel like window dressing. As more women run for office, the rules for spouse involvement will change. Dozens of books have been written about how to run for office, but there is no handbook for how to be the spouse of a candidate. First do no harm is the best motto and remember that everything in the campaign affects them just as much as the candidate.

## Takeaways

➲ Get your plans in order with your family members and close friends first.

➲ The decision you make to become a candidate greatly impacts your family as well.

➲ Keep your plans confidential until you have your ducks in a row and are ready to make an announcement.

➲ Ask your closest friends to head up key roles.

➲ Ask people to join your campaign committee—include all your "circles".

➲ Set up committees to cover all the important campaign tasks.

➲ Identify and solicit help from candidates and elected officials in your area.

➲ There's a social component to campaigning—make it fun and they'll keep coming back.

➲ Be cognizant of the role of your spouse and make sure the lines of communication are kept open throughout the campaign.

# 3

# Personal Financial Impact

*"We must stop thinking of the individual and start thinking about what is best for society."*
Hillary Clinton

While our democracy is open to anyone from any background running for office, there is a personal financial cost in running for office. Personal finances should not be an obstacle, but a realistic assessment of the expenses and disclosure requirements is an essential step to take early in your decision process.

Effective candidates need to begin their campaigns earlier than ever before, which can mean nearly two years of additional personal expenses and campaign fundraising.

## Know the Election Laws

If you are running for a federal office such as U.S. Representative or Senator, you will be required to complete a financial disclosure statement that will include your personal income sources, investments, property and business ownerships and overall net worth.

Many state and local offices do not require full financial disclosure of its candidates, however, ethics and conflict of interest statements are required for most offices that often include disclosure of business ownerships but not necessarily personal financial net worth.

In today's world of political campaigns, there are candidates who run for office that are extremely wealthy, as well as candidates of moderate or modest means. Even a past bankruptcy or financial problems have not stopped candidates from running, but having a secure financial picture is obviously the best foundation from which to get started.

## Personal Inventory

A first step is to take a personal inventory. Assess your personal situation—will you continue to work and receive your income? If you are self-employed or own a business, will the revenue be impacted by your candidacy? Will you take a leave of absence or quit your job?

How much can you contribute to your campaign? Can you fund at least the early costs—the seed money necessary to get your campaign off the ground?

---

*Weigh the costs versus your personal dreams and goals.*

---

Answer these questions honestly, then weigh the costs versus your personal dreams and goals. I know women who have risked it all and others who have made only a modest personal financial investment. It is such a personal decision that no one can tell you that the risks you will take will be worth it. For me it was. I've grown as a person and learned about the political world from the inside; an entirely new world that I was not a part of before I first ran for office, and as a result I've taken a new career path as a political consultant.

**Campaign Finance Laws**

Campaign finance laws are a moving target and vary widely from state to state. Before you even think about whether or not you can afford to run for office and assess your financial resources, check the finance laws first. In some states and for certain offices, there are limits as to how much candidates can self-fund. There are also many variations as to how expenses are reported.

Buying a few new suits might be necessary for your campaign, but is not something you want showing up on your finance report. Get the facts—know the laws. The best place is to begin with your state's secretary of state or your state board of elections. For candidates for Congress, the Federal Election Commission (FEC) governs all political campaign finances. When in doubt, get some professional help—you don't want to screw up these important details.

---

*Buying a few new suits might be necessary for your campaign, but is not something you want showing up on your finance report.*

---

Once you have a handle on the rules and laws in your state, you can proceed with planning the financial portion of your run for office.

## How Much Will it Take?

In 2010, three women running for governor and U.S. Senate ran very expensive campaigns for office. Combined, the women spent over $217 million, much of which was self-funded. Despite a down economy, 2010 was a record-breaking year in terms of the money spent on political campaigns. Races for Congress range anywhere from $500,000 to several million dollars. It is not unheard of for U.S. Senate and gubernatorial elections to cost well in excess of $10 million. Former Senator Hillary Clinton ultimately spent $6.4 million of her own money when she ran for president and spent over $200 million total in the primary election.

Even candidates running for mayor or statewide office are sometimes spending millions of dollars to become elected or retain a seat.

When Houston Texas Mayor Annise Parker won her election in 2009, she spent just under $1 million on her campaign. Stephanie Miner, the first woman elected mayor of Syracuse, New York, spent over $450,000, mostly on television advertising.

In my first race for city council, I spent less than $2,000 for yard signs, stickers, t-shirts and brochures; all self-funded. Fast forward to a different scenario in my 2008 senate race; where more than

$650,000 was spent, of which more than $350,000 was money that I raised. My campaign war chest for the state senate seat began with $5,000 that I personally contributed to pay for initial expenses.

When Jill Miller Zimon first ran for Pepper Pike City Council in 2009, she spent a total of about $5,000 and contributed $3,250 of her own personal funds to the campaign.

It takes roughly $5,000 to get started, covering such items as setting up a website, printing contribution envelopes, palm cards and invitations for early fundraisers. Without these basic tools, it is very hard to kick off your campaign and begin to raise money.

**Getting on the Ballot**

Ballot access and nomination rules increase the cost of running for office. In states where ballot access laws are in place, candidates must secure a certain number of signatures before their name will appear on the ballot. Every state has some sort of nomination process that generally includes obtaining signatures before a name can be placed on the ballot. In some states, the process is quite extensive and money is required to help secure the signatures needed.

States with difficult ballot access laws include Oklahoma, North Carolina, Georgia, Texas, Virginia and Indiana. In Virginia a candidate for statewide office must obtain 10,000 signatures from registered Virginia voters in order to appear on the ballot. It is recommended that 15,000–20,000 signatures actually be obtained to cover bad signatures. Virginia also requires 400 signatures from each of the 11 congressional districts that require extensive travel across the state. Gas, hotel and other travel expenses can add up quickly.

Bart Frazier, Director of The Future of Freedom program, says this about Virginia's daunting ballot access law, "Someone with a political machine to aid him would have to work full-time for months just to get the necessary signatures. He might even have to quit his job."

Be sure to factor in the cost of securing signatures when making your financial assessment before running for office. Contact someone who has previously run for your office to learn more about how to secure the nomination requirements you will need to run and become the nominee.

## The Little Extras

All the little extras you will need to pay for during your campaign can add up quickly. Knowing what those are heading into the race will help you budget and realistically assess the personal investment required. Extra items, outside of the campaign budget, include:

- Clothes—suits, comfortable shoes, parade outfits, walking clothes
- Photography—you will need professional quality photos to start out for your website and publicity *(do you have a friend who is a photographer?)*
- Tickets—for banquets and events to network and meet voters
- Meals—with your on-the-go schedule, there will be little time for eating at home
- Gas—you will put thousands of miles on your car, and gas costs can add up
- Meetings—buying coffee or lunch for big donors you are meeting with
- Hair—good haircuts and occasional stylings will be needed for public and television appearances
- Home entertaining—campaign meetings and volunteer sessions held in your home will cost money to provide refreshments to volunteers (cookies and coffee)

## Sacrifice

When it comes down to it, there is a personal sacrifice to be made, and unless you are willing to make it, this might not be the time in your life to run for office. But if you willing to give it your all and make the personal financial sacrifice that is necessary, you will join other brave women who risked everything to become elected and make a difference.

Ayanna Pressley took a huge personal risk when she made the choice to run for Boston City Council in 2009. Because of the demands of the campaign, she left her job working as an aide to Senator John Kerry. It became necessary for Pressley to cash in her 401k personal savings to pay for living expenses while running for office. Her gamble paid off when she was elected and became the first women of color ever to be elected to the Boston City Council in its 100-year history.

Jennifer Brunner gave up her shot at a likely second term as Ohio's Secretary of State to run for the United States Senate. The seat became open when George Voinovich announced he would not run for another term. Brunner had a strong track record of turning around Ohio's corrupt election system and was even recognized with the John F. Kennedy Profiles in Courage award in 2008. Brunner asked herself "When was the last time a woman was viable enough in Ohio to compete for the U.S. Senate?" Despite the governor's handpicked Lt. Governor entering the race, she decided to go for it, setting up a primary contest.

Despite being financially out-raised in her primary election, Brunner lost but received a very respectable 45% of the vote. It was too late to run again for Secretary of State; Brunner walked away empty-handed, but had built a grassroots following that will be there when she makes her next move.

Kentucky state senate candidate Julie Smith-Morrow put considerable time and personal funds into her 2010 campaign. Smith-Morrow served as a school board member and took on a long-serving incumbent senator who had never been challenged in 16 years. The odds were long that she could win, but her focus on giving voice to the issues that had been ignored for years was worth it to her to sink over $20,000 of personal funds in the campaign in the final weeks to help get her message out. Smith-Morrow lost her election but believes she did make a difference.

"I have no regrets about being defeated pretty soundly. Anytime the voters don't have a choice in an election is a bad thing. It was the right thing to do," says Smith-Morrow. "We represented the people that needed to have a voice and got some very important issues out there."

## Takeaways

⮱ Assess your personal financial situation before making your decision.

⮱ Estimate personal expenses at the beginning of the campaign.

⮱ Be prepared for full personal financial disclosure.

⮱ Learn the finance laws in your state and for your particular race.

⮱ Learn the nomination and ballot access rules for your race.

⮱ Fully estimate costs associated with getting your name on the ballot.

⮱ Don't forget the little extras.

⮱ Be prepared to make a personal financial commitment to your race.

# 4

# Work/Life Balance

*"I always try to balance the light with
the heavy—a few tears of human spirit in
with the sequins and the fringes."*
*Bette Midler*

While at times running for office can seem like it is your entire life, it is not your entire life. In fact, running for office must be included along with all your other responsibilities. Balancing your work and career, family, community and religious involvement and other personal responsibilities while running a political campaign for public office is another challenge that is unique for women candidates.

"I did give up sleep and expended a lot of anxiety over making sure that everything was exactly as I wanted it, especially when I made mistakes and needed to correct things. I also didn't work out or exercise nearly as much as I should have," describes city councilwoman Jill Miller Zimon. Zimon was elected to the Pepper Pike City Council in Ohio in 2009.

While in the national spotlight, Sarah Palin was criticized when she was the Republican Vice Presidential nominee because she had young children still at home, including a special needs infant. Some questioned her parental values to be running in such a high-profile election that would take so much time away from her young children. How could she balance her family responsibilities with her duties in office if elected? Men are never asked that question.

Congresswoman Debbie Wasserman Schultz (D-Florida) was first elected to the Florida House of Representatives at age 26 and has three young children. She has had to answer tough questions about her parenting values serving in Congress with three children. Her husband shares the parenting responsibilities and her children can be found at times in her office in Washington, D.C. In 2011, Wasserman Schultz was named chair of the Democratic National Committee.

After you've taken your personal inventory and had the talk with your family and closest friends, you still must assess your personal physical and mental strength before embarking on your campaign journey. It takes a tremendous amount of energy, passion and commitment to run for office, and as much time as you can give.

---

*How could she balance her family respon-sibilities with her duties in office if elected? Men are never asked that question.*

---

For former Lexington Kentucky Mayor Teresa Isaac, her first race was a county-wide race for an at-large seat on the Lexington City Council. She had her own law practice and two small children, ages seven and four. "I divided my days into thirds—one-third for the family, one-third for my law practice and one-third for the campaign," says Isaac.

## How Much Time Will it Take?

Running for city council, school board or other local office generally can be done with a small campaign budget. Most of the work can be done on weekends. The larger the geographic area and number of voters in your race, the more time that is required. The big question is always, how much time? I only know what it took in my campaigns and how much time other women have spent—there is no hard and fast rule.

Running for city council in my first race was a comparatively short campaign. The filing deadline was in August, and the campaign season officially began after Labor Day. I produced a brochure hand-out and purchased some yard signs and knocked on just about every door in the city on all day on Saturdays and Sundays after church, in September and October. We also campaigned at the local high school football games handing out stickers and shaking hands. No other events, no candidate forums or public appearances were required. During the weeks, I made phone calls to friends throughout the city for help with yard sign locations. I made most of the "asks" for yard sign locations myself, and my husband helped put up signs.

Basically I walked neighborhoods knocking on doors for about 17 full days until close to dinner time. With just seven precincts, that covered it.

For a county-wide or state legislative race, it takes more time primarily because of fundraising requirements and the larger area to cover for direct voter contact. During my first campaign for the senate, I worked full-time and kept my job through the entire campaign, using vacation time for the final two weeks and personal days for some afternoon call time during the summer and fall.

## Here's what a typical work day looked like:

- 7:30 a.m.—Head to work.

- 10:30-10:45 a.m.—Make calls to campaign staff, supporters, and volunteer captains regarding organization and schedule.

- Noon-1 p.m.—Working lunch at my desk making fundraising calls on my cell phone (don't use your company phone).

- 5:00 p.m.—Leave work, go home, change clothes grab a banana or yogurt and head out for knocking on doors until about 8:30 (7 p.m. as it began to get dark earlier- don't walk in the dark by yourself). Grab something unhealthy to eat on the way home.

When I got home, I generally wrote fundraising and volunteer thank-you notes before going to bed. Not being a great sleeper, it was even more difficult during the campaign. Extra stress, ideas and just the pressures of the campaign woke me up many nights at 2 a.m. I used light sleeping medication on nights before big events or debates so that I would have adequate sleep. For me that worked. Every candidate needs to find what works for them, develop a routine that includes some semblance of a healthy lifestyle.

On some evenings, instead of knocking on doors, I attended events, fundraisers, banquets and near the end, debates and candidates forums. On weekends I began walking at about 10 a.m. until nearly 5 p.m. If there were festivals on the weekends, I attended those on Friday and Saturday evenings. In the fall, Friday nights were football games at various schools throughout my district.

*My personal life was basically on hold until after the election, and I was willing to make that sacrifice.*

I began my door-to-door walking campaign right after Memorial Day, and I kept this schedule from May up until Election Day. Sunday was the only day I didn't campaign until after Labor Day. In September and October, I campaigned seven days a week.

It was not much of a healthy work/life balance, but I knew it was only temporary. In fact there was barely time to do laundry, shop for necessary items and food, get my hair cut or go to the dentist. My personal life was basically on hold until after the election, and I was willing to make that sacrifice.

Having lived through this schedule, I would not recommend it for very long. If at all possible, work must be cut back in order to spend more time fundraising and to achieve a better work/life balance. I was totally exhausted and despite being on the go all the time, I gained weight from eating more fast food and living such an unhealthy lifestyle.

## Creating Balance

As women, the great multi-taskers, we can do it all if necessary. The smart thing is to simply ask for more help with the personal things. My husband was very supportive but he was handling a lot of the campaign communication and contact with volunteers and staff, and trying to take care of whatever household duties he could. Our sons were away at college and our daughter was a sophomore in high school and was very self-sufficient by that point, but describes that year of the campaign as "a lot of fun but glad when it was over."

Looking back, I should have taken a little more time off from work. I should have asked friends and family to help out with some healthy meals from time to time. I should have not been so obsessive about knocking on every door. At the time I felt I had to work 110% of the time so that on Election Day, I wouldn't feel that I could have done more. Next time I will be better at gaining commitments from family and friends about what they can do to help my schedule.

"Women have such good organizational skills but are sometimes fearful they can't handle the rigor of a campaign," says Mayor Teresa Isaac. "Women shouldn't be afraid to take the risk because the strength of their organizational skills will help them run great campaigns."

How you handle your work/life balance is a personal choice. I can tell you that if you get more help at home, you will be a more balanced and effective candidate.

## Takeaways

➲ During the campaign, your life will be out of balance.

➲ Be sure you have the physical and mental strength to run for office.

➲ Don't let others question the choices you make about your lifestyle.

➲ Plan your work/life/campaign schedule and stick to it.

➲ Build in a strategy for healthy eating and sleep schedule.

➲ Organization is key to keeping everything balanced.

➲ Speak up and ask for help—be specific with your requests.

➲ Ask for more help at home.

*Pink Politics*

# Part II

## Going For It

*"As a college intern in the Governor's office working on pay equity... I came to understand the political process. It was de-mystified for me. What had previously seemed so complicated was now understandable and I gradually began to think, "Hey, I can do that!"*
*U.S. Representative Tammy Baldwin*

Now that you know what it will take to run for public office, and after you've made the thorough assessment of your life and made the decision to run, how do you get started? Where do you begin, how much money will it take and where will the money come from? Who runs the campaign and how do you craft a message that will resonate with voters? These are all questions that are answered in this section.

5

# Choosing The Right Office

*"Whoever decides to dedicate their life to politics
knows that earning money isn't the top priority."*
*German Chancellor Angela Merkel*

You may be absolutely certain about which office you want to run for, or you may not be so sure. You may not even know all the possibilities that are out there. Determining which office to run for takes considerable thought and research. Not only do you have to find an office that suits you, but it must be a viable race. Once you identify an office that interests you, or perhaps an unexpected opportunity pops up due to an open seat or vacancy, take the time you need to determine if it is a good fit. The organization She Should Run, in their resource book *The Companion Notebook*: *Making the Decision to Serve*, offers some tips about how to find the right office:

- Research job descriptions
- Identify a political mentor
- Read online stories about elected officials
- Read websites of elected officials
- Look for retirements, open seats, appointment opportunities
- Shadow an elected official
- Attend public meetings where elected officials speak

Unless you are an extremely well-known or a high-profile person with a built-in, large base of potential donors, it is best to run for a local or county office before jumping into a congressional or guber-natorial election. You need to prove yourself to the voters before they will support you for a higher office. I've seen many high quality women run for Congress or a statewide office before they built their reputation and created a network.

A very outspoken woman ran in the U.S. Senate primary in Kentucky in 2010 in her first race for public office. I remember think-ing what a great candidate she would be for a local county office. Lacking real political experience and contacts outside of her region, she ended up only receiving 5.5% of the vote. I don't believe in sacrificing women to run in races that are not realistically winnable. If you're going to run, be in it to win, not to make a name for yourself. It is pretty hard to get people excited about your next race if you weren't a credible candidate the first time out.

I was a much better candidate for state senate after first being elected and serving on a city council. Once on council, I had the opportunity to attend related organization meetings, forums and events that helped me expand my network. These contacts helped tremendously when I was ready to take the next step.

As an example, it is typically better to run for a district court judge seat before jumping in and running for state supreme court, and better to start by running for city council or commission before running for mayor.

There are exceptions, but generally a candidate needs to have a deep resumé, strong network and access to money to win a statewide or congressional office the first time they run for public office.

## Which Office Suits You?

At the local level, a variety of offices are filled with elected officials. Visit your local election or secretary of state website for specific details including filing information, rules for holding office including

minimum age and residency requirements, and whether an office is

partisan or non-partisan,

## Potential Local or County Elected Offices

| | |
|---|---|
| Circuit Clerk | Judge-Executive |
| Clerk of Courts | Magistrate |
| Commissioner | Mayor |
| Committee Member | Property Valuation Administrator |
| Controller | Register of Probate |
| Coroner | |
| Councilwoman | School Board |
| County Attorney | Sheriff |
| District/State Attorney | Supervisor |
| Equalizer | Surveyor |
| Jailer | Township Trustee |
| Judge | |

## Potential State or Federal Elected Offices

Agriculture Commissioner

Assemblywoman

Attorney General

Auditor

Commerce Commissioner

Councillor

Court of Appeals

Governor

Insurance Commissioner

Lt. Governor

President

State Representative

State Senator

Secretary of State

State Supreme Court

Superintendent of Public Education

Transportation Commissioner

Treasurer

U.S. House of Representatives

U.S. Senate

## Appointments and Special Elections

Appointments and special elections are another way to seek public office without going through a typical primary or general election. Appointments are made by mayors, top county officials and governors. Typically, appointments to local office must be ratified by members of councils or commissions.

Federal and state laws dictate how appointments to offices are conducted when a vacancy occurs during the term of a public official. Most federal and state laws allow for an appointment to be made until the next regular or a special election is held. Governors have the special power to appoint a person to a U.S. Senate seat if there is a vacancy, but the public must elect a member to the House of Representatives if a vacancy occurs. This is done by special election unless the next regularly scheduled election is a short time away.

Local party officials also can be involved in partisan races if they are required to submit a nominee for a special election. In addition to submitting an application or letter of interest for a vacant elected position, it is important to contact the leader of your local or state party for additional information if the position you are seeking is of a partisan nature.

Natalie Tennant (D-West Virginia), was elected in 2008 as West Virginia's Secretary of State at the age of 41. When Governor Joe Manchin was appointed to the U.S. Senate after the death of Robert Byrd, Tennant filed as a candidate for governor in the 2011 special primary election. She lost that election to the appointed governor but was able to return to her Secretary of State position since she did not have to give up her office to run for governor.

If you have identified an open seat appointment for public office, the next question to ask yourself is "will an appointment to the seat help or hurt your chances to run for the seat in the next election?" Mayor Elaine Walker of Bowling Green, Kentucky resigned her seat as mayor to accept a gubernatorial appointment to serve as Secretary of State. While taking on the responsibilities of a new high profile office, she was faced with a heated primary election within five months of accepting the appointment. Walker lost her election and will leave office just one year after giving up her position as mayor.

Two women attorneys were both appointed by the governor to judicial positions and began immediately serving as judge while running highly competitive campaigns. Both were able to use their judicial title and status while running for office, but both women were defeated by opponents who were able to campaign full-time instead of presiding over court every day. "While it was difficult to take on a new job and begin a campaign at the same time, I believe having the position of a judge helped me gain credibility as a candidate," says Kathleen Lape, former Kenton County Kentucky District Court Judge.

Other women have accepted appointments and gone on to win their elections to keep their seats. In many ways, there is a distinct advantage to being the incumbent office holder when it comes time for the next election. Talk with previous office holders, local political experts and party officials before you seek or accept an appointment to a public office.

---

*Becoming an elected official is not as glamorous as it may seem... exposing yourself to public scrutiny is also part of the job.*

---

**Public Service**

Becoming an elected official is not as glamorous as it may seem. Running for office is one of the highest forms of civic engagement and public service, but is extremely time consuming and demanding. Exposing yourself to public scrutiny is also part of the job.

Before deciding which office you will be running for, make sure that you are willing to dedicate yourself to the office when you win after the campaign. Are you willing to make yourself available to citizens to take their phone calls and help them with problems and issues? While the rewards can be many, the personal sacrifice required is significant. It is because of the sacrifice of our true public servants that citizens hold them in high regard.

Princeton Kentucky Mayor Gale Cherry believes it is important for women to have established a reputation of community and public service in order for the voters to be receptive to you as a candidate. "It is crucial to have established yourself and have developed a reputation for getting things done," says Mayor Cherry.

**Takeaways**

⮡ Do research to determine what it takes to hold your desired position.

⮡ Build upon your track record and experience to determine best fit.

⮡ Start local or regional unless you have exceptional connections and qualities.

⮡ Make sure you meet all eligibility requirements before filing.

⮡ Follow filing instructions to the exact specifications.

⮡ Seek an appointment if a seat is vacant and you can handle the election requirements.

⮡ Be prepared to commit yourself totally to become a great public servant.

# 6

# **Getting Started**

*"I want history to remember me not just as the
first black woman to be elected to Congress, not as the
first black woman to have made a bid for the presidency
of the United States, but as a black woman who lived
in the 20th century and dared to be herself."*
*Shirley Chisholm*

D uring the early days while you are still trying to visualize yourself as a candidate, and again after you've settled on which public office to run for, more questions than ideas surface.

"Next time I would rely less on Washington consultants and more on my own instincts," says U.S. Senate candidate and former Ohio

Secretary of State Jennifer Brunner. Asked about what she would do different next time, Brunner says "I would strengthen my grassroots campaign and spend less early in the campaign."

This is excellent advice. Spend very little money during the early months of the campaign. The best approach is to spend at least 2–3 months making the rounds. Visit with and get to know the movers and shakers in your community. Spend time listening to advice and learning about the issues that are important.

If you are running for city council, have coffee or lunch with other council members, the mayor, city administrator, fire chief and other community leaders. You can tell them you are exploring a run for office and would like to hear their thoughts. Since people love to talk, you will have no problem extracting valuable pearls of wisdom and an insider view of the important issues.

Remember to do more listening than talking. It is important for them to get to know you, but it is just as important that they think you are someone who cares about the issues and what they have to say.

Unless you are lucky enough to have politicians in your family, it is important to include local experienced candidates and political operatives among your campaign team, if only for advice. Solicit the help of candidates, especially women, who have run in your area. Find out from them what worked and what did not, and what it will take to win in your geographic location.

---

## *Remember to do more listening than talking.*

---

If you are running for state legislature, you will need to speak with other legislators within your party and region, caucus leadership, political party leaders, former elected legislators, community and business leaders. Do your homework and spend the time you need to build relationships with important individuals. They'll be sizing you up as well, so always put your best foot forward—first impressions are huge in politics.

Whenever you meet someone, be sure to ask "Who else do you recommend that I should meet?"

"It is especially important to focus on building your campaign team before launching the operation," says Brandon Thorn, political consultant with Dark Horse Campaigns. "Fundraising is the key to any campaign's ultimate success and is especially important when running against an incumbent."

## Skeletons in Your Closet?

Women candidates are more fearful than men of things in their past coming back to bite them or causing embarrassment if they run for public office. When a female candidate has opened up to our consultants about something they were worried about, it generally was not the sort of thing that would cause harm in a campaign.

The best course is to discuss issues and fears with your campaign consultants, strategists or key supporters to allow for complete vetting of the potential obstacle. A good strategy to deal with the obstacle early in the campaign can avert trouble down the road.

## Skeletons That Can Be Overcome

Adultery
(unless caused recent scandal)

Arrest
(depends on what the offense was)

Bankruptcy
(unless running for treasurer or financial office)

College pranks

Divorce
(unless multiple times)

Drunk driving
(can be overcome if it was a long time ago)

Fired from job

Gay or gay relative/child
(never a skelton but can be an issue)

Kicked out of school
(must have been a long time ago)

Participated in college protest

Past alcoholism or drug problem

Quit or fired from job

Single parenthood
(can be an asset)

## Skeletons That Can Be A Problem

Arrest for violence

Drunk driving
(if recent or repeat)

Can't hold a job or never worked

Professional misconduct

Caught lying in public

Pornography or inappropriate sexual conduct

Abandoned or gave up custody of child

Hate speech

Financial mismanagement

Inappropriate sexual photos out in public

Christine O'Donnell, 2010 Republican U.S. Senate candidate from Delaware, made considerable headway in her election despite several potential skeletons in her closet. O'Donnell's 2010 run was her third try for the same office in five years. She also had recent financial trouble and failed to make payments on her mortgage for her home. The house was ultimately sold at auction, which lead to a messy IRS claim. The Citizens for Responsibility and Ethics in Washington (CREW) accused O'Donnell of making false statements on FEC filings and illegal use of campaign funds as her "own personal piggy bank."

O'Donnell turned this negative around and used it as a way to connect with voters who were also having financial problems due to the economic conditions. Despite her baggage, O'Donnell beat her opponent in the Republican primary and garnered 40% of the vote when she lost in the general election to Democrat Chris Coons.

## Opposition Research

Sophisticated and well financed campaigns conduct opposition research or background checks on their opponent as well as a background search on their own candidate. The following information can be gathered during a professional opposition research project:

- Legal background—lawsuits, bankruptcies, corporate filings, civil and criminal court records, military records and employment disputes.

- Campaign finance (if opponent is an incumbent)—analysis of industry ties, PACs, inappropriate contributions.

- News search—news articles, public statements/quotes, letters to the editor, memberships.

- Incumbent voting record—past legislation, vote history, position testimony, constituent communications, flip-flops and broken promises.

After the research is performed, a notebook is prepared that includes all of the information in chronological order to make it easy to refer to for polling and campaign messaging.

"Messaging, strategy and targeting are shots in the dark without proper research," says Rick Svatora, Partner with S&W Capitol Advisors national research firm.

On doing research about yourself, Svatora quotes Sun Tzu, "If you know the enemy and know yourself, you need not fear the results of a hundred battles." Svatora uses the motto "know thyself" when it comes to advising candidates about whether or not to spend the money for self-research.

In my second senate race, our opposition research showed us that my opponent had spent his 12 years in office filing only religious and anti-abortion legislation. He failed to address education, the economy and jobs. We used a strategy that blamed him for failures on the economy and budget.

In a race for Congress in Kentucky's 4th District, a former congressman had written a letter asking for leniency for a prison sentence for a constituent who had mishandled bank funds and was convicted of fraud. Obtained through opposition research by his opponent, the letter surfaced and became the basis for a damaging series of attack ads during the campaign.

Opposition research costs can range from about $3,000 for local and county-wide offices to $7,000–10,000 for larger campaigns. If you cannot afford to hire a professional, ask a friend who is an attorney or an internet-savvy student to spend some time researching your opponent's public and legal history.

Knowledge is power. You need to know as much about your opponent's background as possible. There will be opportunities when

you can use information you have learned to help frame your opponent's positions or message during the campaign.

**Making your announcement**

There are several ways to make your formal announcement—distributing a press release, holding a press conference or rally, standing
on your capitol steps (if a legislative run), or recording a video and
distributing it online through email and social media. Whichever
method you choose, use the opportunity to get some free media
coverage and make a big splash for yourself. Get used to tooting your
own horn.

Remembering to spend very little in the early stages of your
campaign, so unless you are going to use your announcement as an
opportunity to raise money, do not spend anything on an announcement event.

**Securing Commitments**

Be sure to ask whoever encouraged or helped recruit you to run
specifically what they will do for you during the campaign. Don't
settle for a vague answer like "Oh, I will be there to help you" or "Yes,

I'll help you raise money." Pin them down and don't let up until you have a specific answer.

Here's an example of a good ask, "This is a big campaign, I'm going to need a lot of help and want to know specifically what I can count on you to do."

Here's an example of a specific good answer, "I will help you raise money by calling some of my friends and neighbors and inviting them to a neighborhood fundraiser at my home." To which you respond, "That is wonderful, how much do you think you could raise at the event you will host?" The person should give you a specific amount, but if they do not and say something like "Gee, I don't know, I've never done this before." Then you say "Would you accept a goal of $2,500 and try to line up hosts with pledges to get us to that amount?"

After the financial goal is set, then you should ask, "Would you be willing to host the fundraiser in the next 60 days?" After their answer, work to secure a date and put it on your campaign master calendar. Have your fundraising consultant or staff member take it from there to line up the details, plan the event and send out invitations.

It is extremely important to get some campaign cash flowing in quickly by lining up some financial supporters in the very early stages. There is more about how to put together a fundraising plan in chapter eight.

## Early Election Issues Strategy

To develop a strategy, start with big picture questions and narrow down to specific issues—what would you do if you could run the world? What top three areas will you focus on? What are the hot issues surrounding your race and your constituents?

Even if you are running for school board or county clerk and there is not a single big issue that everyone is talking about, you still need to develop a strategy to allow voters to identify with you and your message.

Strategy can be developed through different sources. It is important not to confuse overall strategy with message. From *Winning Campaigns* political consulting group, "The essence of political strategy is to concentrate your greatest strength against the point of your opponent's greatest weakness."

When I ran for city council the first time, I had attended and participated in council meetings for a year before I even thought about running. After that experience, I came away feeling that the council didn't listen to the concerns of our neighborhood. Too much resistance to change, new ideas, and doing things in new ways. My strategy when I decided to run was to contrast myself to the "old guard" way of doing things and that I would be a change candidate who would listen to the voters and try new things.

I know a single mother of four who ran for family court judge, whose strategy was easy—she could relate to the voters on family court and domestic issues because of what she has been through raising four children on her own. Her opponent was a traditional, political establishment candidate who seemed out of touch.

Congresswomen Kathy Hochul (D-New York) won a special election as a Democrat in an extremely Republican district. Her strategy was to focus on Medicare and her message was simply "Save Medicare, vote for Hochul." Building upon her opponent's message of reducing Medicare benefits and the national mood at the time, Congresswoman Hochul's strategy was to take the one hot issue and turn it into her campaign message.

Former Texas State Representative Ellen Cohen used reaching out and listening at neighborhood meet-and-greets as her primary campaign strategy when she ran for Houston City Council. With a broad community and civic background, Cohen used the face-to-face meetings to allow people to get to know her and so that she could learn more about the needs of the citizens.

**Takeaways**

➲ Ask yourself the tough questions.

➲ Spend time early talking and listening to movers and shakers.

➲ Don't spend much money early.

➲ Line up key individuals as supporters.

➲ Determine if you have any *real* skeletons in your closet—prepare a strategy to deal with them.

➲ Gather as much opposition research as you can.

➲ Plan your announcement and start raising money.

➲ Secure specific commitments from supporters.

➲ Develop a campaign strategy for how you will win.

# 7

# Running Your Campaign

*"Women are more likely to think…'This is going
to be tough. I don't know how to do this. I've
never done this before. I am not sure I can do it.
So I need all the help I can get'."*
*Center for American Women and Politics*

Today's campaigns are sophisticated operations, run with technology and experts in polling, fundraising, messaging and field operations. Depending on the size and budget of your campaign, critical functions can be performed by consultants, staff or volunteers. Backroom operations including your donor database, voter files, website and social media are key and among the first expenditures necessary to running a professional campaign.

The first slot to fill is that of your campaign treasurer and compliance officer. This can be a volunteer but needs to be someone who understands and can file your finance registry reports accurately and on time. Some candidates are able to secure an accountant to take the role. Both the treasurer and candidate should take advantage of state-provided training and workshops to help them with finance and compliance issues. Even innocent mistakes can become major campaign issues.

Additional staff members and consultants can be added at the beginning (or later) in your campaign depending on your needs and budget. Campaign staff and consultants are hired to help formulate and then implement the strategy to win the election. Small or low-budget campaigns often fill many of the jobs with unpaid volunteers. Campaign services can be performed by hiring staff or securing consultants to serve as experts in various areas. Again, affordability is often the driving factor in making the decision to hire outside people. Talk to others who have run and won before you make your decision about hiring staff or consultants. Meet with as many different people as possible.

Look at the area where you are weakest personally, whether it is in fundraising, campaign organization, or operations, and bring on board a person or consultant with that expertise first. Additional staff or consultants can be hired once your budget is established and fundraising is well underway.

Most important is that the candidate herself does not become bogged down in the details that can easily be handled by staff, consultants or volunteers. The candidate cannot be the campaign manager, but should have the opportunity to approve important messaging, photography and budget expenditures throughout the campaign.

---

*Most important is that the candidate herself does not become bogged down in the details that can easily be handled by staff, consultants or volunteers.*

---

Those of us who are control freaks often have a hard time letting go and allowing others to carry our message. As a candidate you should be involved in developing the strategy, setting goals and determining the budget (both revenue and expenses) but allow others to handle the execution.

Remember the cardinal rule for candidates—if you are not raising money or speaking with voters, don't do it!

**Professional Fundraisers**

Professional fundraisers assist the candidate by developing a budget and finance plan. They keep the candidate focused on contacting high-dollar donors while finance committee members can help secure low-dollar commitments. In my first campaign the only full-time person I could afford was a fundraising consultant. He ended up providing much more than fundraising and was a critical member of the political strategy team. This decision was the right one for me because at that time I felt so inexperienced in political fundraising that this would be the most important hire I could make.

**Campaign Manager**

The campaign manager is the lifeblood of the campaign. The campaign manager is the coordinator and director of the day-to-day operations of the campaign. The campaign manager directs staff and works with consultants on behalf of the candidate. An important duty of the campaign manager is to direct how the candidate spends her time. Providing adequate fundraising call time, working to help coordinate events and fundraisers and plan and provide tools for the grassroots portion of the campaign. The campaign manager should not necessarily be the "body person" or staff the candidate for every function, but is the person who makes the trains run on time.

In larger campaigns, there will be others who work for the campaign manager, but often, the campaign manager is the only paid staff person. That can mean their role expands to take on field operations as well as communications.

## Communications Director

Your communications director can be a paid consultant or staff person, or a volunteer who works in public relations or marketing. Make sure you have someone who understands politics and can devote the time to working with your strategy and campaign team in order to craft messages that are in line with your overall strategy.

The communications director is responsible for press releases, working with the media and bloggers, writing speeches and talking points, posting articles and comments on the campaign website and handling social media sites such as Facebook, Twitter, LinkedIn and Google+. She or he should also be responsible for communicating with local and state party communications directors to disseminate press releases and talking points for party websites, newsletter and television and radio interviews.

The communications director should provide the information to the candidate on candidate forums and debates, prepare speeches to be given within allotted time frames, and provide talking point hand-outs as needed at forums.

## Field Organizer

The field organizer is one of the last members to be added to the team because the bulk of their work is in the final four to five months of the campaign. Their primary responsibility is to organize and map a field plan, and managing volunteers and paid canvassers for a targeted direct voter contact program. Too often, candidates overlook this critical function and set out on a mission to talk to every voter by knocking on each and every door in the district or county, a hugely inefficient waste of valuable time and resources.

The field organizer will develop a field strategy that includes a program for the candidate herself—typically talking to voters that are considered "persuadable". He or she will develop a plan for volunteers to identify or build support for the candidate that can include a more broad targeted universe. Finally, they plan and execute the get-out-the-vote (GOTV) efforts in the final two weeks before the election.

In key races, field organizers can be brought in by a party organization that will eliminate the need by the campaign to hire field staff in the final months. For congressional and gubernatorial campaigns, field operations is a large undertaking and candidates in other down-ticket races can benefit from the efforts of the field campaign.

A targeted field plan is essential when planning a program that includes both the candidate and a small army of campaign volunteers.

Depending on the size of your campaign, there are a number of potential roles for professional staff or consultants.

## Potential Staff or Consultant Roles

Direct mail consultant

Media buyer

Media consultant

Opponent tracker

Opposition researcher

Pollster

Scheduling/advance

Technology coordinator

Volunteer coordinator

## Fees and Costs

Costs to hire staff and consultants vary as broadly as do campaign sizes. In general, no more than 20-30% of your total campaign budget should be spent on staff or consultants. The rest should be spent on getting out your message.

When working with consultants and campaign firms, make sure that you know exactly what you are paying for and that are no surprises with costs. Each consultant should work from a specific budget and should seek your approval before incurring any additional expenses, such as sending something to the printer.

As with most things in life, you get what you pay for. Hire the best you can possibly afford. Hire people with experience and a track record of success.

## Volunteers

Friends, colleagues and local party volunteers can fill critical roles in your campaign. Select people you know and trust to take on the most important roles. Set clear parameters and areas of responsibility from the beginning. Volunteers are looking for ways to help your campaign and need to be utilized where their skill set will be most effective.

In my first campaign for the Kentucky senate, we held volunteer planning meetings at my house about a year before the election to begin planning and assigning roles. The volunteer leadership positions in my campaign included committee chairs in multiple areas.

## Volunteer Committee Chairs

Event chair

Fundraising chair

Parade chair

Precinct captains

Teens for Groob chair
(my daughter)

Volunteer chair

Yard sign chair

Young professionals co-chairs

## Sample Volunteer Form

Kathy Groob for Senate

# How You Can Help

**Serve As A Precinct Captain**
If you would be willing to serve as a Precinct Captain, or assist in Precinct level activities, our Precinct Chair is xxxx xxxxxx. Please feel free to contact xxxx directly at 555-5555 or by email at xxxx@xxxxx.com.

**Attend or Host a Fundraising or Meet & Greet Event**
New events are being added all the time. Upcoming events include:
- February 13, 5-8pm, Meet & Greet
- February 25, Fundraising event, 5:30-7pm
- March 19, MainStrasse Event (Groobin' On Main), 6pm-midnight
- March 21, Meet The Candidate Tea, 1-3pm

**Tell 10 Friends and Help Spread The Word**
Word of mouth is our best weapon. Make a list of 10 friends, tell them why you support Kathy and ask them to tell 10 of their friends. Help spread the word by distributing literature and displaying a bumper sticker.

**Keep Your Eyes and Ears Open**
We need people to keep us informed of the issues that matter in your area, and of the activities, positions, and initiatives (if any) of our opponent. Help us stay informed so we can seize opportunities to tell our story as well as respond to misinformation.

**Arrange Meeting and Speaking Opportunities**
If you know of any groups or gatherings of people (large or small) where Kathy can meet your friends, neighbors, and colleagues in an informal setting, or in a formal speaking situation, please let us know.

**Do Competitive Research**
We need people to pore over the legislative record of our opponent, find inconsistencies between public pronouncements and behind the scene actions, review finance filings, and monitor press coverage and events.

**Volunteer for a Committee**
Committees include: Events, Precincts, Finance, Grassroots, Signs, and Volunteer Committee

**Collect Names, Phone Numbers, and Email Addresses of Supporters**
The best, most efficient way for us to communicate with our rapidly growing group of supporters is via email and the web. Help us build our list by collecting names and contact information of supporters.

**Recruit A Young Person**
Young people are our future. Make a difference in the life of our community, and recruit a young person to get involved and engaged in the political process.

*If you would like to volunteer for any of the above, email jeff@kathygroob.com or call 555-5555. Please continue to visit our website for the latest information, and to sign up for events and activities.*

### www.KathyGroob.com

Paid for by Kathy Groob for Senate, Barry G. Kienzle, Treasurer.

Don't overlook involving high school students in your campaign. Some students are required to fulfill political service hours for a social studies or civics class. Young women are often excited to be involved with a female campaign and it is a great way to provide them with exposure to politics, so that someday they too might become politically active and perhaps eventually run as a candidate.

Remember that volunteering in a political campaign is in many ways like getting behind your favorite sports team. There is a social component and it is very important to make sure you build in opportunities for your volunteers to have fun and socialize together throughout the campaign. We held periodic coffees, cocktails and cookouts to help bring the volunteers together. Just don't let having fun detract from the real campaign work!

## Takeaways

➲ To run a professional campaign, you need professionals.

➲ Begin with a strong treasurer/compliance officer.

➲ Look at the areas where you are weakest, such as in fundraising or organization, and bring on that person or consultant first.

➲ Additional people and consultants can be hired once your budget is established and fundraising efforts are underway.

➲ As the candidate, do not become the campaign manager—delegate, let go!

➲ Hire the best you can afford; you will get what you pay for.

➲ Hire for your most critical areas; utilize volunteers to cover other functions.

➲ Start off with a well-organized team of volunteers and leaders.

➲ Don't overlook young people—they have great energy and ideas.

➲ Make the campaign fun so that volunteers will stick with you throughout the entire time.

# 8

# Raising Money

*"Women candidates have two unique problems.*
*They have trouble raising money and being*
*taken seriously by the media."*
Maureen Reagan

The most dreaded and distasteful part of every candidate's run for office is raising money. The thought of having to ask people for money, especially friends, family and even people you don't know is frightening. In working with candidates, I've seen the good, bad and ugly of fundraising. So much has been studied, written and taught when it comes to political fundraising that this entire book could be about just about fundraising.

Yes, it is true, women often have a harder time raising large amounts of money because they often do not travel in the money power circles of their male counterparts.

"There are governors and senators who still hate fundraising," says Loren VanDyke Wolff, attorney and former political campaign manager. "They never get used to it, which is ok, but it has to be done. Eat your broccoli!"

The bottom line is that without enough money your campaign is doomed from the start. The key word here is *enough*. It's not necessary that you outraise your opponent. It is certainly possible to develop such a strong grassroots and volunteer organization that you will not need a massive budget to win, but you must have *enough* cash in the bank to be seen as credible and to support your messaging campaign.

If there is time before you launch your campaign, attend training for fundraising. Organizations such as EMILY's List, The White House Project and Emerge America offer training, but not in every state. Private companies offer video and webinar training as well.

My advice to first-time candidates is to hire a coach. Hire an experienced fundraising consultant or staffer who will be committed to helping you develop a finance plan, budget and goals and to keep you focused on fundraising each and every day throughout your campaign.

## Obstacles to Raising Enough Campaign Cash

Candidates who are not effective at fundraising generally fall into one or more of the following categories:

- *Avoiders*—cancels call time appointments, uses call time for other tasks, never has enough time to do it.

- *Yakkers*—shoots the breeze with donor prospects and friends and never gets around to asking for a contribution.

- *Scaredy cats*—makes the calls but just cannot muster the courage to ask for a specific amount, won't ask people for specific commitments.

- *Promisers*—promises to make calls on their own, but results and cash never come.

- *Long Shot*—a race that is so one-sided that no one thinks you have a chance to win; make sure you are in the right race at the right time.

With or without a coach or consultant, fundraising efforts should begin on day one and continue until the final week of the campaign. There is no more powerful ask than the candidate herself making the request for financial support. Others can help, but the candidate ask is essential to success.

Candidates sometimes self-fund a portion of their campaign, but it is not necessary to ensure success if you are willing to develop your skills and become a fundraising champion.

## Start at the Beginning

It's always best to start with a plan that includes targets and specific goals for raising money from the following sources:

- Candidate call time
- Finance committee efforts
- Events
- Party organizations
- Political Action Committees (PACs)

Once you've established goals by month for the various money sources, *you, as the candidate running for office* are ultimately responsible for soliciting funds and commitments from all the sources. You will need to identify and ask key people to serve on your finance committee. You will need to line up hosts for most of your events and will need to participate in interviews with PACs and political party organizations in order to receive their financial support.

Help from finance committee members and supporters is great, but don't count on it. It is your campaign, your finance plan and your responsibility to see that the money is raised.

**Donors**

The best source for raising money is from people you already know, and from traditional donors who have given to other candidates throughout the years. We call this your low-hanging fruit. Go after the low-hanging fruit first, to build your coffers and leverage success into contributions from those outside your personal circles.

---

*The best source for raising money is from people you already know.*

---

In the following Donor Circles graphic, it starts with you in the middle and your closest donor prospects, and radiates outward to those farther away from your reach and thus harder to secure.

**Donor Circles**

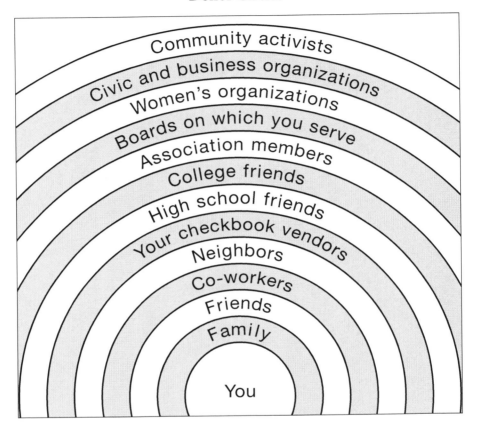

**Building a Donor List**

Gathering your donor prospect list is a bit like building your first

backyard tree house. You need to gather pieces and parts from every-

where. Even if your consultant or staff member provides you with a political donor database or list, you should add to it with your own lists.

Here are some possible sources for beginning to build a good donor prospect list:

- Alumni lists and high school yearbook

- Christmas Card List

- Church/Synagogue or school directories (depending on how localized your race)

- Outlook or other personal database

- National, state and local political finance databases (such as www.opensecrets.org)

- Previous candidate donor lists

- Women's club memberships/organization lists

Now you know why I've suggested that you get started early on your campaign. Sorting through potential donor lists and entering their contact information into a database can be quite time consuming. In many cases, it's an early do-it-yourself project until you have some help. Cultivating prospective donors is an on-going process that will continue throughout the campaign as you meet and hear about new, interested people.

"Your donor list will become your most cherished political asset," says Loren VanDyke Wolff. Keep a clean and accurate list from the beginning.

Resources are available for managing lists or a simple spreadsheet will suffice until you can purchase a database program or hire a consultant that provides database services.

## Finance Committee

For judicial candidates and on up the ladder to someone running for Congress, finance committees can make the difference between raising some money or actually raising enough money to win. If you can gather at least 10-20 of the most influential and powerful people in your community or region to serve on your finance committee, it helps lend credibility and resources to your campaign.

You will need a strong finance chair or co-chairs to call the group together and keep the focus on making calls and gaining sponsors for fundraising events. The campaign should provide donor call lists, but each finance committee member should be prepared to bring their own list of people they are willing to call on your behalf. The best results come from each member having and committing to raise a specific amount.

My finance committee meetings were held at my house with campaign staff present to note the decisions and target calls to be made. The campaign should take as much of the administrative work off the shoulders of the team members so that their primary focus is on making calls. Even with a finance committee member calling a specific donor prospect, it is still important for the candidate to follow-up on a pledge and give each donor the attention and respect they deserve.

---

*Gather at least 10-20 of the most influential and powerful people in your community or region to serve on your finance committee...*

---

**Fundraising Tactics**

In business, promotion is based on the marketing mix. In politics, the fundraising mix is the variation of actions you must take to raise cash. As discussed earlier, personal solicitation by the candidate is the most effective with the highest rate of return of any method for raising money. During a 10-month or longer campaign, a variety of methods can be used to bring in cash on a regular, steady basis.

Candidates should make calls for amounts of $250 and up. For lower contributions and for re-soliciting prior donors, direct mail, email and telemarketing can be used to raise money.

Solicitations should always include an easy way for donors to contribute. Mail programs and event invitations should include a remittance envelope. Emails should include a highly visible, easy-to-find contribute button. For a first-time mail campaign using a good source list, expect about a 1% response rate and slightly higher (5-10%) rates for a re-solicitation mailing. Email campaign response rates are similar but slightly lower.

By comparison, direct face-to-face or telephone solicitation by the candidate will yield a 30-75% response rate. You can count on events yielding 10-25% of your targeted revenue.

During my campaign, we invited all donors to every campaign event and fundraiser. It was remarkable to see the number of people who became repeat contributors, even giving as many as seven or eight different times throughout the campaign. Lower dollar donors can become significant because of the consistent contributions they give over the course of the entire campaign. Many women outside the political arena that are not accustomed to contributing to campaigns often end up becoming consistent, repeat donors.

---

*Personal solicitation by the candidate is the most effective with the highest rate of return of any method for raising money.*

---

Creative themes and messaging with regard to fundraising can help improve your rate of return. Women's events featuring chocolates have been known to bring in crowds, and special guest speakers and entertainers can also impact your success (but only if they volunteer to perform for free).

The young professionals group in my senate campaign organized a pub crawl and called it "Groobin' on Main." It was held in an entertainment district within the largest city in my district and included stops at seven pubs and restaurants. People paid $25 to attend, received discounts on drinks and most purchased a special commemorative t-shirt for $20. It was a huge success in terms of fun and momentum, and we raised a several thousand dollars with very little expense.

**Call Time**

"Having dedicated call time is the single most important aspect of a successful fundraising operation," says Brandon Thorn, Dark Horse Campaigns political consultant. "My client Miriam Paris outworked her opponent in the call room and raised more money. Paris spent at least four hours every weekday on the phone calling donors. She ultimately raised $70,000 during her three-month special election, while her opponent was busy putting out yard signs and raised only $15,000."

Women, being the highly organized creatures we are, need everything ready and conducive to success when sitting down to make fundraising calls. Most likely your finance database will be electronic, but many women still like a fundraising notebook that they keep with them and use when fundraising.

The notebook system should be organized so that there are individual call sheets that include all of the prospects' contact information and previous contribution history by candidate, date and amount. The notebook should also have two additional tabs to divide the calls already competed from the calls still to make. In addition, some donor prospects will need to be placed in a future "call again" tab in the notebook because they prefer to wait until later to contribute to your campaign. I called some people six or seven times before achieving success.

Use a script to help you remember all the important points you need to cover, and use individual call sheets or files to make notes about leaving a message, when to call back, and the response you received.

Ask for a specific amount based on the person's campaign contribution level history or what you believe they can afford to give. Start high because you can always reduce the amount of your request. If you ask for $1,000 or $500 and get push back, try a lower number. Just make sure you nail down a specific amount even if it is $50. Most prospects who use the line "I will send you something," generally do not. Your goal is to get to a level that is comfortable to the prospect and secure a firm commitment.

Follow-up is critical. Send a follow-up letter confirming the pledge including a remittance envelope the same day. Make a note of when it was sent, and call back as a reminder if you don't receive a contribution within two weeks. Best practice is to ask your donor to make their contribution by credit card on your campaign website. If you have staff or a consultant to perform the follow-up mail function, then you will be available to make more calls.

Remember, when making calls to prospective contributors, you are not begging for money. You are giving people an opportunity to support and share in your vision for the future. Many donors see it as a investment and a chance to do something positive for their community, state or country.

**Scripts**

When calling prospective donors for money, there are several critical elements that will ensure your success. Success points are easy to forget when you are actually on the telephone in the midst of a conversation, so a script will help you remember all your talking points—just be sure to use the script. A good consultant sits with you during call time. They will help you stay on track as well as handle the notes and follow-up.

Your script should be printed in large type on one sheet of paper that is in front of you at all times during the call. Start by introducing yourself, then deliver a customized message that shows how your prospective donor will benefit from having you in office.

Move on to the reason for the call, state what you need, why and a specific amount. Be sure to say that you can win if you have the resources to get your message out. Create a sense or urgency, wait for the person to respond, then you respond accordingly.

The closing is just as important as the introduction. Be sure to confirm the action to be taken, state the responsibility on your part— picking up a check, sending an envelope or repeating the website address *again* for an online contribution.

## Sample Cold Call Script

*Hi, this is Janie Smith and I'm running for the Kentucky Senate against Fay Jones. She has repeatedly voted against jobs for our state and is part of the obstructionist leadership in the Senate. I'm calling to ask for your support for my campaign to create jobs and to put a stop to this type of dysfunctional government. Will you support me by making a contribution of $250 to my campaign?*

**If yes:**
*You can contribute online by credit card at www.electjanie.com, or would you like to send a check? (If yes to check, offer to send an envelope.)*

**If no to $250:**
*Would you be able to make a smaller contribution, perhaps $100 or $50.*

*If yes, write down name, amount, and verify email address. Tell them you will send a confirmation and all the details.*

## Sample Event Call Script To Line Up Hosts

*Hi, this is Janie Smith and I'm running for state senate against Fay Jones. We are having a campaign fundraising event on May 7th and I'm calling to ask if we can list you as a host for the event at Tom and Tina Black's home?*

**If yes:**
*Our co-host level is $500, is that something you are comfortable with?*

**If no to $500:**
*Would you be able to participate at the sponsor level at $250?*

**If no to $250:**
*Would you be listed as a friend at the $100 level?*

*If yes, write down name, and verify email address. Tell the host you will send a confirmation and all the details.*

## Finance Reports As Deadlines

Depending on the race you are in, you will have finance report deadlines that are dictated by your board of elections, state registry of election finance, secretary of state or the Federal Election Commission (FEC). Accuracy in your compliance with these reports is important, but what makes them even more valuable is that they are wonderful self-imposed deadlines for achieving fundraising goals.

Your finance consultant or expert will help you identify all the dates that are critical to your fundraising goals. Pay particular attention to the early deadlines because your performance will be closely watched and judged, and will impact your future fundraising ability.

Reporting deadlines are useful when making calls to prospective donors, especially to those who are regular political donors and with whom you have already established a relationship.

## Sample Finance Deadline Script

*Hi, this is Janie Smith. I want to let you know that with your support, I can win the state senate seat in November. An important campaign finance report is due on October 1st. Would you help me meet my goal by contributing $500 to my campaign?*

**If yes:**
*I am happy to pick up a check from you today or you can make a credit card contribution on my website.*

**If no:**
*Would you consider helping me with a smaller contribution of $250 or $100? Thank you so much for your support.*

*If yes, write down name, amount, and verify email address. Tell the donor you will send a confirmation and all the details.*

## Fundraising Events

The number one rule of political fundraising events is to keep your expenses to a minimum, in order to maximize the amount of cash you actually put in your bank account. I've seen far too many candidates and their hosts pour hundreds and even thousands of dollars into events and then realize at the end that they only raised a couple of hundred dollars after all the expenses are itemized and paid.

Political fundraisers should be lean and quick. They are not parties; their sole purpose is to raise money. The best times are weekday evenings beginning from approximately 5-7 p.m. Most people will stop by, deliver their check, have a drink and maybe a nibble or two, then head out the door.

The best events are hosted at someone's home, with the host supplying and paying for the refreshments so that every penny raised goes into your account. Campaigns will often pay for invitations and postage in order to ensure that the process is handled properly and that an adequate number of targeted guests are invited. Be sure to include the cost of your host's expenses as an in-kind contribution; check out your local rules.

"Events can be a huge success when held in a different type of venue where a supporter has agreed to in-kind the space," says Dark Horse Campaigns political consultant Brandon Thorn. "Music clubs, comedy clubs and art galleries are other non-traditional venues to hold events."

Cocktail receptions, dessert and coffees and hot dog grill outs all serve well as fundraising event gatherings. Events take planning. You will typically need at least six to eight weeks in order to properly plan and promote a successful event.

I always sent flowers the day of the event to the person hosting my fundraising event. It is a nice, inexpensive touch to let the person know how much you appreciate their kindness.

## Your Event Plan

Secure a host, date, time and location

Develop a host committee

Determine the budget; be candid with your host about
keeping expenses to minimum; ask if they are willing to make
an in-kind contribution of the food and beverage costs

Collect an invitation list from host and
host committee if possible

Design, print and mail invitations
(approximately 2-3 weeks before event)

Make calls to invited guests issuing personal invitations

Send email reminders to invited
guests and post on social media

Prepare for registration, money and greeting table

Use name tags to help remember people's names

Prepare brief candidate remarks—recognize
elected officials and other dignitaries in attendance

Thank your host and host committee
along with all your supporters

## Saying Thank You

This is one area in which female candidates excel. I often get this question, "should I send out thank you notes for contributions from an event even if I thanked the audience in person?" The answer is *yes*—always, always send thank you notes.

Showing your appreciation, especially with a personal note, goes a long way toward building a good relationship with your donors and will help increase your repeat contributions throughout the campaign. It also goes a long way towards building your network.

Several female candidates I know used a pre-printed thank you card and included a personal thank you message and signature. Following events you might have a large stack of notes to write, so allow yourself a couple of weeks to write the notes and mail. I found that later in the evening before going to bed was a good time to write thank you notes.

## Sample Thank You Note

*Thank you for your generous contribution to my campaign.*

*You've brought us a step closer to giving the people of*

*our state the leadership voice they deserve.*

*With your help, we will have the ability to bring our*

*message of change to the voters this fall.*

*I deeply appreciate your support and encouragement.*

*(hand signed)*

**Takeaways**

⮑ Without enough money, you don't have a chance.

⮑ Hire a coach, consultant or experienced staff person.

⮑ Don't procrastinate or avoid doing the job.

⮑ Identify your money targets and monthly goals.

⮑ Create a good donor prospect list from various sources.

⮑ A strong finance committee can make a huge difference.

⮑ Candidate call time yields the best results.

⮑ Be organized when you sit down for call time.

⮑ Use a script to stay on track.

⮑ Finance reporting deadlines are good benchmarks.

⮑ Plan events carefully keeping expenses low.

⮑ Always, always send thank you notes.

# 9

# Effective Messaging

*"Even though I felt I was the most qualified
candidate in the race, I needed to raise money so
I could get my message out to voters."*
*Oregon State Senator Kate Brown*

C ampaign messaging is an industry buzz word, but it is simply this: telling your story and why you are running for office in such a way that it convinces voters to support you. While you are focused on your ideas, passion and message, the average voter does not have a clue what is going on politically and who is running for what. Don't take it personally, but citizenship isn't what it used to be in the United States and frankly, people are too busy with their daily lives to be concerned with what you have to say. As a candidate, you need to find a way to get through to them.

"Most people do not spend a lot of time thinking about politics. They spend their time thinking about their own lives so if you try to force them to listen to too much they will not hear anything. The best messages are not only simple but very repetitive," says Doug Heyl, media consultant and owner of Scout Communications.

The secret to great campaign messaging boils down to three things:

1. Knowing the important issues and what will persuade voters,

2. Simplifying your message into one that voters can understand; and

3. Money.

Without enough money, your message goes nowhere.

I have listened to novice candidates say things like "I want to focus on my message and don't need to spend all my time raising money." Or, "We will focus on grassroots approaches to getting my message out." Bunk!

Without enough money candidates cannot print door hangers or cards (with a message on them), can't do direct mail pieces (with a message on them), cannot run radio or TV ads (with a message on them) and cannot respond when attacked by their opponent.

If you don't believe me, go back and read the last chapter again. Here are the keys to effective messaging:

## Key #1: Know The Issues

If you can afford it, make the investment to conduct an issues/benchmark poll in July or August to determine how voters are feeling, what issues are important and if they've heard of you or your opponent. Polling is always determined by your campaign budget, and if you can't afford to put at least 6-10 times the amount of money you would spend on a poll towards delivery of your message, then you probably cannot afford an issues poll.

Without good hard polling data, you will need to rely on your own instincts and feedback you extract from voters in your district. Low-budget ways to capture information on issues include putting a survey on your website and promoting it by email, volunteer phone calling using a questionnaire, or conducting a do-it-yourself focus group where you gather voters together to ask them questions. Most importantly, candidates need to understand their community, state or district better than anyone.

Once you have obtained the information you need, you can begin to craft your strategy and message. Again, if you can afford consultants to help you with this, great. But if not, count on friends who might be in the marketing or political business. Trust your gut when it comes to how you will speak to the voters and allow your message to develop throughout the process. For example, you may notice that certain issues consistently arise when talking to voters at the door or at events or when speaking with donors.

## Key #2: Simplify Your Message

It is important to understand complex policy issues, but don't obsess over them or feel you need to master every talking point. When I ran for the Senate the first time, I lived in fear that I would be stumped by a question from a reporter or voter on some issue that I knew nothing about. I created notebooks, studied every night and crammed in complex talking points on issues that never even saw the light of day in my campaign. It was like cramming for a test—I could pass but couldn't fool anyone. The lesson is stick to what you know.

Simplify! You don't need to be a master of all subjects. There are a few critical issues that you will need to master. Learn and listen to people who know the most about those issues, but craft your message simply and in a way that will be understood and resonate with your voters. Nobody expects you to be a master of all issues, but you need to know the really important hot button issues and be able to talk intelligently to the voters.

**Effective Messaging Words**

Leadership

Trust

Change

Progress

Conservative

Values

## Key #3: Money

You've already read the fundraising chapter, but it is important to know where to spend your money on getting out your message. Some candidates waste money by spending it too early on things that don't help get you votes. Of your total campaign budget, at least two-thirds should be spent on messaging in the final weeks of the campaign.

That means if you begin in January for a campaign in November, there is very little spending other than for basic supplies and staff until August, September and October.

Make your best assumption about how much money you will raise, then create a campaign budget that includes all your basic expenses, saving the majority of the funds for messaging in the fall. Avoid spending pitfalls like nail files, tote bags, buttons, barbecues, DJs, note pads and campaign apparel. None of these items spread your message or earn you votes. They are money-wasters and you can win without them.

It is more advantageous to go deep than to spread your dollars thin. If you are running in a smaller or local race, spend all of your messaging dollars on direct mail and a phone program rather than trying to do a little each of mail, phones, billboards, radio, and cable TV. When beginning a radio or television campaign, the budget must be large enough to gain repetition value from running your ads. Honest political consultants will advise you about how many gross rating points are needed to get your message out effectively in the area in which you are running. Do not take advice from amateurs on this subject.

## Response to Negative Messages

Even though most campaigns start out with a civil tone, eventually they always work their way into some sort of negative attacks or even downright lies about you, your record and what you stand for. It is important to stay focused on your strategy and not let every negative message seep into your psyche or worse, knock you off your message. A good opponent will try to define you, but don't let him!

Representative Susan Westrom knocks on every door throughout her entire district during the campaign season and uses those face-to-face opportunities with voters to respond to lies and smears that her opponent is using against her. She simply asks the voter at the door "When somebody lies to get in office, what do you think they are going to do when they get in there?"

"The people who are most upset by negative smears are your family," says Westrom. "Candidates develop a thick skin and it is more important to stay on your message."

## Which Medium?

Should you sink your precious campaign dollars into television, radio, telephone messaging (robo-calls), direct mail, outdoor (billboards/bus cards) or other smaller message venues?

Ideally, if budget allows, television advertising will allow you to reach the most people. Doug Heyl says this about political television advertising, "good political TV does two things: the first is that spots need to be up longer with more GRP (gross rating points), and the second is good spots look different and sound different than political spots of the past. Television is both a visual and audio medium so you have two chances to grab the viewers attention by sight or sound. If you grab their attention then you have a much better change for your message to work."

---

*A good opponent will try to define you, but don't let him!*

---

Heyl also believes that low-budget campaigns can benefit from cable TV if the area and district they are running in have efficient cable systems. "All good TV buys now have cable networks as part of a buy and depending what time of year cable can really be a good buy," says Heyl.

"The biggest problem with low-budget campaigns and television are the production costs," says Heyl, which can run from $2,500 to $10,000 per spot. "Very good television ads can be made with still photos and stock footage. For a cable buy to penetrate you need at least 250 spots a week for 4 weeks on stations targeting your demographic targets. Cable is a slower burn medium than broadcast television (major networks), so length of time one can be up running ads should play a role in deciding if cable television works in your campaign budget."

Radio works in some markets but is not as effective as it used to be since more and more people are listening to satellite radio and iPods. Radio is still the choice of many candidates and should be at least considered in the mix of your campaign messaging dollars.

## Slogans

Finding the right message and boiling it down to a three-word slogan is no longer a difficult early campaign task. A helpful website offers free lists of slogan ideas with just a click of a mouse. (Visit ElectWomen.com for links). Categories of slogans include themes like change/results; experience/trust; town/community; choice/vote/elect and school/law enforcement.

I credit the slogan I used in my first city council race for my success in coming in second in a field of 15 for eight seats. My city council slogan was *First, She Listens*. It was on everything—my signs, stickers and handouts. Long after the campaign was over, I still received calls from constituents asking if I was the "lady who listened."

Here's where I formed the idea behind the slogan. Several neighbors and I attended a city council meeting to ask the city to step up patrols and add speed humps for a dangerous crosswalk on our street in front of the local school. After sitting through the lengthy council meeting and listening to the shallow deliberation, we walked away empty-handed. Mostly we felt that the mayor and council members weren't listening to us.

When we left the meeting, my neighbors turned to me and said "you should run for council." I thought about it, took my personal inventory, and said to myself "I know I can do a better job of listening to the citizens."

Angie Strader, a female candidate for Property Valuation Administrator (PVA) in rural Kentucky, utilized her mother as her chief campaign strategist. Her mom came up with Angie's slogan for PVA—*Please Vote Angie*. It was very clever, simple and it caught on. If you don't have a campaign strategist mom to rely on, the professional consultants are very good at this sort of thing.

Slogans matter. Especially in small races where there are fewer funds to get your message out. Early polling is best to help you settle on a great theme, but without that, use your best judgment, bounce it off some of your supporters, then go with a strong message and slogan—and stick with it!

### Takeaways

⮕ Develop a message that connects with voters.

⮕ Keep your message simple.

⮕ Use polling to learn what issues are important to voters.

⮕ Stick to what you know and master the key issues.

⮕ Spend majority of money in final weeks make smart media buys.

⮕ Don't just dabble in advertising—repetition is what counts.

⮕ Develop a great slogan and use it consistently.

*Pink Politics*

# Part III

## Secrets To Winning

*"It doesn't matter what I say about an issue, if I have a run in my pantyhose, that is all anyone will talk about."*
*U.S. Senator Blanche Lincoln*

In every venture, there are those who stand out. The special people who radiate light in everything they do. Call them winners, lucky or even charismatic. But more often than not, they are working harder, are more prepared and more courageous than the average person.

*Pink Politics*

# 10

# Outwork Your Opponent

*"A Congresswoman must look like a girl, act like
a lady, think like a man, speak on any given subject
with authority and most of all work like a dog."*
*Representative Florence Dwyer*

T ime and time again I've spoken with women candidates who
won their elections against all odds. These include women
that ran in a district that had a history of voting for the opposite
party. There are many examples of women who did not have much
in terms of resources winning their election despite the odds. There
is a common thread among those who pulled upsets or nearly won a
tough race, and it is that *they outworked their opponent.*

Despite coming up a half a percentage point short in my last election, I like to think that I outworked my opponent and that I was the better candidate. My opponent was an older man who frankly was tired of running for office and was used to coasting. He did very little while in office, or during his campaign. Extreme partisanship helped keep him in office; and my hard work brought me within a very close margin of winning.

---

*There is a common thread among those who pulled upsets or nearly won a tough race, and it is that they outworked their opponent.*

---

What hard-work strategies and efforts have women used to push them over the finish line on Election Day? They mostly include a lot of shoe leather and persistence. "At the end of the day, these races are still about shoe leather, door-knocking and pancake breakfasts," says Tim Storey, senior fellow at the bipartisan National Conference of State Legislatures. "You can still outwork your opponent."

Outworking your opponent means virtually a 16-18 hour a day campaign and working smart by spending your time focused on two areas — fundraising and talking to voters. Sounds simple, but what does that really mean?

Working smart means showing up at the right events, meeting and speaking with as many voters as possible, and slipping out before long speeches begin or a banquet dinner. Some evenings I attended three events, making sure to touch as many voters and donor prospects as possible, but careful not to engage in lengthy policy discussions and campaign chatter. You will need to learn the art of "touch and go", which is to making contact and fully engaging with a person but then moving on in order to cover an entire room.

Former candidate and attorney Eric Deters, in an article titled *The Perfect Candidate*, says "you don't have to be perfect, just outstanding." In sports, the hardworking candidate would equate to "Charlie Hustle". You need to be energized and hustling every minute of every day.

Teresa Isaac credits the hard work she displayed while on the campaign trail as a big factor in her election as mayor of Lexington Kentucky. "Voters saw me as accessible, saw my boots on the ground and saw me as a person who would listen to them both as a candidate and as mayor," says Isaac.

Use every spare moment for making money calls and lining up meetings with large contributors and influencers. Early morning coffees or breakfast meetings can be squeezed in before work or before call time. Find time to call neighbors and friends to ask if they will host a house party or meet-and-greet so you can expand your circle of friends and donor prospects.

Depending on your regional and geographic dynamics, the campaign season will include several different types of events where large crowds gather. Good voter contact events include Lenten fish frys, church festivals and picnics, holiday parades and events, senior picnics and bingos, back-to-school events and parades, state and county fairs, food festivals, and fall harvest festivals and events.

"A campaign at this level was a really serious undertaking; you need to work hard to get all the support you can," says Kentucky Senate candidate Julie Smith-Morrow. "It's a huge undertaking and it's not something you can do well unless you give it 110–150%. You have to be committed to going all the way and really believe in yourself. It was probably one of the hardest things I ever did."

Showing up at everything contributes to the "buzz" and the chatter that builds around your campaign. Political activists and party insiders know when a candidate is working their hardest and will reward their effort by engaging and spreading the word.

Field strategists will tell you that door-to-door voter contact is the most effective way to directly communicate with your targeted voters. It is not unreasonable to expect a good candidate to spend 5-8 hours at a time knocking on doors. Festivals and other summer and fall events should not get in the way of targeted voter contact. I was able to spend the weekend days going door-to-door and then visiting events and festivals during the evenings.

Even experienced candidates dread the drudgery of walking door-to-door, day after day. But like going to the gym, it feels great once you are there and doing it. Connecting and talking with voters is what politics is all about.

"I knocked on every door and really connected with people," says Mayor Gale Cherry of Princeton, Kentucky. "You need to do more listening than talking and find something you have in common with the people you are speaking with. Everyone has different circumstances and if you can share something in common, they will relate to you as a candidate," says Cherry.

State Representative Susan Westrom used a grassroots strategy to win her first election for the House seat she won in 1998. "I was able to cover every door in my district twice and I also had friends who were dropping literature for me, but I knocked on every door," says Westrom.

## The Little Things Do Matter

Hard-working candidates are remembered most for the connections and special kindnesses they offer their constituents. After my door-to-door walking, on Friday nights during high school football season, I campaigned at the football games handing out zip-loc bags of peanuts that included campaign stickers on each bag. It was great fun because my football game volunteer would hand out the bags to families waiting in line for their tickets and say to them "You would be nuts not to vote for Kathy." It always brought a laugh and was a fun, friendly way to connect with strangers.

There was one instance that a child was unable to accept our bag of peanuts because he was allergic to peanuts. Once the game began and our peanuts were gone, I purchased a bag of chips at the concession stand, put one of my stickers on it and found the child sitting in the stands with his parents. He was thrilled to have the potato chips, but more than that, his parents were impressed that I had taken the time to bring him something he could eat. I'm a mom, so taking care of a child's needs came natural to me. I'll never know if that family voted for me or if they told anyone else to vote for me, but it felt like the right thing.

Representative Susan Westrom carried small bags of dog biscuits with her while canvassing for those occasions when a dog greeted her at the voters' door. She also distributed bumper stickers for voters to put on their garbage cans with the hope that at least once a week her stickers would blanket the district. "People don't always want to put stickers on their cars and trash cans were a perfect place to build name recognition," says Westrom.

Candidates are often invited to attend bingos and other activities put on by senior citizens so that they have a chance to meet and talk with interested voters. Believe me, seniors are interested and most do vote. Don't attend a senior bingo or other activity empty-handed. Take the time to purchase some little goodies to bring along, attached, of course, with a campaign sticker or card. Cheese crackers, cookies and other nibbles are a big hit as well as any bakery item. Some seniors suffer from diabetes, so do not bring only sweets.

Some candidates distribute note pads, nail files, jar openers, fans and other trinkets which are always popular because people like to get free stuff. Don't spend precious campaign dollars on trinkets, but if you have someone willing to donate or provide the items at a substantial discounts as an in-kind contribution, then by all means take advantage of the opportunity.

## Personal Notes

The more personalized a message, the more likely it will help you build a connection with a voter or supporter. Many evenings I spent handwriting messages on post-it notes to leave at the doors of voters who were not at home when arrived at their door. I attached a post-it note to my door hanger that read something like this:

*I'm sorry I missed you today. Your vote is important to me and I am available to talk at your convenience at 555-555-5555. (signed) Kathy*

Our campaign also took the time to personalize yard signs when they were delivered. Messages were printed on a piece of paper and cut into 3"x 4" pieces. We taped the message shown below to each campaign sign, and when they were delivered, the sign was placed in the yard and the note was taped on the door.

*Thank you for your support for Kathy Groob for Senate. If your sign becomes damaged or stolen, or if you have a friend or neighbor who would like a sign, please contact the campaign at 555-555-5555.*

This little extra touch encouraged supporters to take ownership of the sign and helped the campaign with replacements so that key locations were always covered.

**Going the Distance**

The last few days before the election are generally spent in a frenzy of GOTV efforts and canvassing. There is very little persuasion that can be done in the final days, and the nerves of candidates are about shot by this point. By all means, candidates should keep walking, but if there is late money to spend and some rainy days, the best use of those last-minute dollars is a persuasion ID touch-pad telephone poll that will identify undecided voters and a list for the candidate to follow-up with calls or visits. Here's how it works:

- Identify a universe (example: 3,000 independent voters).
- Automated calls are placed using your final campaign message plus asking voters if you can count on their support on Election Day.
- If they say yes or no, toss them away. If they are unsure or undecided, they are flagged on a list for the candidate to call.
- Candidate spends the mornings of the final 3-4 days calling the undecided voters.

Just the act of calling someone personally, letting them know how important their one vote is, will bring them over to your side. Believe it or not, the final few days are when many voters finally start to pay attention.

Candidates who have taken this extra step swear it makes an impact in their race. The ability to identify undecided voters in the final few days, and then making personal contact with them, is the highest and best use of money and the candidate's time.

Never stop until the polls close.

### Takeaways

⮕ You can win by outworking your opponent.

⮕ Winning is about door-knocking and pancake breakfasts—attend everything.

⮕ Focus on two things—fundraising and talking to voters.

⮕ Master the art of touch and go—meeting many people at an event and not getting stuck, but making people feel you are focused on what they are saying.

⮕ Squeeze money calls and lining up meetings in between work and events.

⮕ Spend 5-8 hours each day knocking on doors for at least 3-4 months.

⮕ Get creative for getting attention at events—give out lots of stickers.

⮕ Bring giveaways for bingos and senior events (cheap food, not expensive trinkets).

⮕ Personalize your door-to-door literature and yard signs.

⮕ Make persuasion ID follow-up calls in the final days.

# 11

# Grow A Thick Skin

*"Let me tell you, sisters, seeing dried egg
on a plate in the morning is a lot dirtier than
anything I've had to deal with in politics."*
*Ann Richards*

In some ways there is nothing you can do to prepare for devastating news, so let's put this politics stuff into perspective. Devastating news is loss or death of a loved one, divorce, your house burning down, serious injury or illness of your child, kidnapping, violence… I think you get the picture.

Politics has a bad reputation, and the fear of negative campaigning scares many women away and keeps them from running.

Professor Jennifer Lawless from the American University Women in Politics Institute says that "You know you are taken seriously as a candidate and credible when you come under scrutiny. A thick skin is developed quickly and it's not something you focus on much when you are running."

Most negative campaign attacks are not nearly as rough as they seem. Probably your advisors are telling you to "get a thick skin". What does that mean? Put on some artificial coat of armor or stick some ear plugs in your ears? Be a big girl? (I hated when some of the male politicos would say that to me—I am not a girl!).

It's all rubbish. First of all, it's never really as bad as it is made out to be. Second, the only way to develop a thick skin is to gather some scrapes and scars to toughen it up. In other words, the thick skin develops from taking some of the attacks, handling them the best you can, and becoming better and stronger as each attack ensues.

Sound scary? When Franklin D. Roosevelt said "You have nothing to fear but fear itself," perhaps he was talking about campaigning. The negative smears, attacks, and innuendos are only as bad as you allow them to become. It's how you handle them that makes the difference for you as a candidate.

If you allow a negative smear or trick to seep into your psyche, it can paralyze you, knock you off your game and dampen you and your supporters' enthusiasm.

---

*The only way to develop a thick skin is to gather some scrapes and scars to toughen it up.*

---

You will need to learn to pull back your shoulders, get a stiff upper lip, and stay focused on what you should be doing—talking to voters and raising money. Staying positive, confident and secure is where you need to be especially during the final weeks of a campaign. When it gets hard, just keep repeating to yourself—sticks and stones, sticks and stones. Sticks and stones will break my bones, but words will never hurt me.

*Stay focused on two things—talking to voters and raising money.*

**Be Prepared**

I was a Girl Scout and the motto "be prepared" was drilled into me, so let's get you prepared for the negative part of the campaign—the tricks and mudslinging. The more you know, the better you will be able to handle the distractions when they come at you. *That's all they are—distractions.* Little mini-dramas that get in the way of a focused campaign.

In political campaigns, there is nothing quite like that first attack. It's not devastating, but it can certainly be disturbing. Below are various types of political attacks that can knock you off your game *if you let them.*

## Campaign Tricks

In her book, *...and His Lovely Wife*, journalist Connie Schultz, wife of U.S. Senator Sherrod Brown of Ohio, describes a scene where two men tried to steal garbage from their home. When she reached her husband by telephone to tell him what happened, he replied "I'm sorry honey, welcome to the campaign."

During my senate campaigns, I experienced what felt like dirty tricks designed to intimidate me.

## **Typical Political Attacks**

Attacking your character

Lying about your record

Insinuating something troublesome about your past

Attacking and/or lying about your sexual orientation

Cheating/upsetting you at a debate or candidate forum

Saying something offensive to a member of the media

Forcing you to defend a lie

Negative anonymous robo-calls

Attacking your family/children/siblings

Spreading false rumors about your finances or legal troubles

Putting out anonymous flyers on cars,
doorknobs and in the mail

Sexist remarks

I attended a special event at the Governor's Mansion at the special invitation of Kentucky's Speaker of the House. It was a bipartisan event that included legislators and other special guests. My opponent was there along with the Senate President of the opposition party. Being new to the political scene it was a big thrill for me. It was exciting for me to be there and since I had a nearly two-hour drive back home, I left after staying just about an hour.

The next morning, I received a telephone call from my local daily newspaper political reporter asking me if I was kicked out of the Governor's Mansion. As you can imagine, I was flabbergasted and in shock that someone had made that totally false allegation. The reporter said that a senator (not my opponent) had called to say that I had been asked to leave and escorted out by state troopers. I responded that nothing of the sort had occurred. Even though no story was written, I was rattled to the core and worried that the reporter would think I was lying and had actually done something wrong at the Governor's Mansion.

This incident occurred in January, with the election not until November. I endured 10 months of these sorts of dirty tricks, clearly meant to intimidate me and weaken my position. Every time I thought I was developing my thick skin, they would throw something else at me. What did they think, that I would become afraid and quit?

Another trick came when we were sitting down for an on-camera interview at a cable television station. My opponent and I were seated next to each other waiting for the host to begin the show. Difficult as it was, we were making small talk about the weather and the like. Just moments before the cameras came on, he asked me, "Does your boss know you are taking so much time off work for your campaign?" Boom… I went blank. The cameras turned on and I sat there stunned by his question. My mind was racing, oh my gosh, did my employer say something? Was I going to be in trouble?

I quickly gained my composure but I am certain my responses to the questions were not as sharp as they would have been otherwise. How could they be? I had a million other things racing in my mind.

I was a Vice President at a real estate development firm during the time of my election and had the full blessing of my employer. The cable television interview that I was participating was being held at noon, during my lunch hour. I had nothing to worry about, but I was unprepared to be confronted by my opponent with a question of that type, and so I was indeed rattled.

Have your guard up the moment your opponent or any of his operatives are within your sight. Don't let anything they say get inside your head; better yet, just ignore them and stay away.

Kathleen Lape ran for election to district court judge in Kenton County Kentucky after being appointed by Kentucky's Governor Steve Beshear. Her opponent had been soundly defeated by a woman in a previous election for judge so he was not going to allow another woman to beat him a second time.

---

*Have your guard up the moment your opponent or any of his operatives are within your sight. Don't let anything they say get inside your head; better yet, just ignore them and stay away.*

---

Judge Lape enjoyed the support of her spouse who happened to be a gynecologist/obstetrician who had a couple of days off each week to devote to her campaign. He became a pro at putting up large signs and was the master of parades, as well as taking care of the couple's two sons and household chores. After a few months of heavy campaigning, it became known that the judge's opponent was out telling voters at the doorsteps that Judge Lape's husband was an abortionist (a completely untrue charge, but a hot issue in the district). The Judge ended up having to explain and defend her husband's profession instead of talking about her qualifications as a judge.

Other common tricks include removal of campaign signs—which are not cheap. Some opponents systematically remove your campaign signs, especially the large expensive ones. They will also have volunteers or staff members go along after you walked a neighborhood and remove door hangers or other campaign materials you might have left behind.

**Bullies**

Sometimes underhanded tactics can come from your own side of the aisle. The party establishment and powerful elected officials tried to get U.S. Senate candidate Jennifer Brunner to shut down her primary election campaign against the sitting Lieutenant Governor. She had successfully won the Ohio Secretary of State election in 2006 and in a short time had cleaned up the election fraud mess in Ohio.

"What they just didn't get, was that I was not getting out," says Brunner. "I had worked hard to gather women supporters throughout the state to build a viable campaign. I could not let the women down and would not let my daughters down. I was staying in the race and would die before I would get out of the race."

Sam Bennett, CEO/President of Women's Campaign Fund and She Should Run experienced quite a shock when she was running in her first campaign for Allentown, PA mayor. It was a three-way primary and she was running against a 26-year senator and a local businessman. She had been recruited by leaders in both the Democratic and Republicans parties to run. The year was 2001.

"It was the first debate in the race and all of the media was there to cover the event," says Sam Bennett. "Halfway into my opening speech, the moderator interrupted me saying 'I was lying in bed thinking of you last night… just what are your measurements?'"

Stunned, Sam Bennett stammered for a few seconds and quickly launched into her platform about fighting crime. Looking back and knowing now that sexism against women should never be tolerated, she took her personal experience to light the fire for her important initiative—*Name It. Change It.*

"We must erase the pervasiveness of sexism against all women candidates—irrespective of political party or level of office—across all media platforms in order to position women to achieve equality in public office," says Bennett.

## Keeping Your Guard Up

At open debates and forums, your opponents' people will attempt to set you up with difficult questions. There really isn't much you can do other than to be prepared and have your own people submit questions that will expose your opponent's weaknesses. Best suggestion is to stay on your message no matter what you are asked, and always bring the discussion back to your talking points and platform.

Also watch out for "mister nice guy". If you are at a public event with your opponent and crowds of people and a person with the opposite camp or someone you don't know is sticking around you being extremely nice and talkative, watch out. They are most likely trying to distract you, keep you from speaking with voters, or might even be secretly filming or recording you.

When in public, always assume you are on camera. In today's high-tech, tiny camera/cell phone world, assume you are always on the record.

## E-Media

Do not allow an email of yours to fall into the hands of someone working against you. Be very guarded in the emails you send out, particularly in response to issues and questions about your background or your opponent. It is best to speak to a constituent in person, or on the telephone, if they have a question about your stance on an issue. Unless you can respond with something exactly as explained on your public website, it's best not to respond in writing. Don't comment about anything controversial in an email and do not hit "reply all" on any emails. Your public statements need to be vetted and aligned with your overall campaign strategy.

*When in public, always assume you are on camera.*

The same warnings apply to Facebook. Go through yours and your family's Facebook accounts and remove any photos you would not want to appear in a campaign ad or mailer against you. Photos with alcoholic beverages, dancing, in a bathing suit or other less-than-flattering shots should be removed long before you enter a race for public office.

Do not comment, tweet or write Facebook posts that do not reflect your image, message strategy, or your public persona. Keep your comments, "Likes" and thumbs up messages to positive, general subjects. Before commenting or "Liking" someone else's posts, ask yourself this question, "Will this help or hurt me with the majority and opposition voters in your district/county/state?"

**Alcohol and Drinking**

This subject is worth discussing in terms of your political campaign and your life as an elected official. I know of two very highly accomplished and respected elected officials who were brought down by mistakes with alcohol. Although these events happened to men, it's important enough to share.

A sitting state senator had a couple of a drinks at a reception before heading home for the evening. He was pulled over by a state trooper and charged with a DUI (driving under the influence). During his next re-election campaign, despite a long history of accomplishment, a negative campaign mailer telling about the DUI hit voter mailboxes the day before the election. It was too late to respond to the devastating attack, and the Senator was defeated by a relatively unknown newcomer.

The next incident occurred when a long-term county clerk who enjoyed strong bipartisan support ran for re-election against an opponent who had contacts inside the clerk's office. Out for an office celebration with co-workers, the clerk left a bar after having a couple of drinks at happy hour and was immediately pulled over by police as his car left the parking lot. It was clear they were waiting for him and most likely someone inside the bar had tipped off the police that the clerk was leaving.

The result was a DUI and embarrassing front page headlines that led to his decision to withdraw from the clerk's race in order to save his family from further scandal and embarrassment.

The bottom line is, if you are running for office, don't drink in public, period. Why take the chance? I'll even go one step further and suggest that your husband, partner, or driver not drink either. It's all too common for someone supporting your opponent to tip off police when you leave an event. Getting pulled over for a possible DUI is most likely a fatal blow to your candidacy and any future political career.

When attending social events, banquets, picnics, skip the wine and beer and drink water, soda, coffee or tea. Do not be photographed with a wine glass in your hand or anything else that looks like an alcoholic beverage. I'm not a big drinker anyway, but sometimes at a luncheon or in the evening I enjoy a club soda on the rocks with a twist of lime. My point is to avoid anything that looks like an alcoholic beverage, even if it isn't. Photos of you, your spouse or other family members with drinks in their hands can be twisted and used in negative campaign mailers. Err on the side of caution and skip the drinks unless you are in your own home or the home of someone you trust with your life.

*Don't let alcohol be the cause of a lost campaign.*

## Political Bloggers

I hope by now you can feel your own skin changing and becoming rougher and thicker. If not, bring on the political bloggers.

Whether friend or foe, bloggers are out there and are growing in number and as primary news sources. Political blogs, negative websites, 527s, you name it, you can count on getting slammed for something in your campaign. The problem is that they are not held to typical journalistic standards and there is no fact checking or truth watch when it comes to online posts and articles. Candidates are fair game and you will have to learn to turn a deaf ear to the negative bloggers.

Another common trend is for opponents to develop a website meant to smear a candidate or expose their record. State Senator Denise Harper Angel of Kentucky learned that her opponent had purchased a domain with her name in it (with a slight modification) so that when anyone Googled her name or typed in the domain name thinking they were getting her website, they got a surprise instead. The site was filled with smears and distortions of her record, and high praise of the man who was her opponent.

527s and political action committees also get into the act by creating their own smear messages, websites and commercials. This became so prevalent during the last presidential campaign that both Hillary Clinton and Barack Obama put up websites to counteract the smears. They tried to set the record straight by publishing their version of the facts.

Perhaps with the list of female political bloggers growing, the environment will become more friendly for female candidates. As of last count, there were 275 women blogging on politics and the list is growing according to Catherine Morgan, contributing editor of *BlogHer*.

## Media Bias Against Women?

Never before has so much airtime and ink been devoted to scrutinizing a female candidate as it was during Hillary Clinton's 2008 bid for president. Women's organizations and Hillary supporters were outraged at how she was treated by the media. The consensus among female pundits and elected officials was that she was held to a higher standard. Some say there is no way any woman, even Hillary, could have run with the record that Barack Obama had at the time.

Was it more than that? Was it misogyny, or just that female candidates are still rare and therefore stand out in the media like the shiny new penny?

As a woman candidate, expect to be scrutinized in ways that you might not expect. Your personal appearance, background, accomplishments and even family lifestyle will all be fair game in your election. Gloria Steinem, co-founder of The Women's Media Center, wrote an op-ed for The New York Times entitled *"Women Are Never Front Runners."* Steinem insists that women are not taken as seriously as men because of sexism standards, explaining "children are still raised mostly by women (to put it mildly) so men especially tend to feel they are regressing to childhood when dealing with powerful women."

*The worst thing to have happen to you by the media is to be ignored. If you are being ignored, you are not seen as a credible candidate.*

Even female journalists have been criticized for using sexist comments that Joan Walsh, Salon Editor-in-Chief says, "Serves to reinforce stereotypes not dispel them." Maureen Dowd used words like nag and witch with regard to Hillary Clinton.

In 2010, a historic collaboration between Name It. Change It., She Should Run, the Women's Media Center and Political Parity turned common political wisdom about how women should handle sexism in the media and in political attacks upside down. Celinda Lake, renowned pollster and consultant to countless women candidates, has stated: 'If we had had this research in Hillary Clinton's presidential race, there might have been a different outcome.' The research demonstrated that even mild sexism, such as focus on hair, makeup, and shoes, is just as damaging electorally, as virulent misogyny.

The research proved that the electoral impact is significant, undercutting a voter's ability to see a woman candidate as likeable and trustworthy. However, as long as a woman candidate immediately responds to sexism in the media or political attacks and calls it sexist, she can not only regain all the lost votes, but also gain a positive bump in the polls from voters who assume her opponent was behind the attack, whether or not that was true. It's equally effective, if the candidate speaks out on her own behalf or if third parties do it for her. Interestingly enough, an equally positive benefit is enjoyed by the woman candidate who either calls it sexist and pivots off that to talk about what voters really care about, or who says right there that it's sexist and stresses that women have classically had to endure such attacks despite the fact that no man would ever have to put up with this. Surprisingly, research shows that both strategies work equally well. The most important thing is that the woman candidate calls it what it is—sexist.

In her 2010 bid for U.S. Congress (VA-01), Krystal Ball used the Name It. Change It. findings superbly. As a challenger who endured sexist photos of herself blasted all over the internet, she ran a terrific race against an entrenched incumbent, but polling showed her still trailing. Polling showed her use of Name It. Change It. closed the margin of loss by over 10 points and turned her into an overnight national and international media pundit—she became the third most Googled name in the world and is now an MSNBC commentator.

Because Ball used Name It. Change It. research to her benefit, she was able to call out the sexist attacks for what they were. Congresswoman Janice Hahn, in a special election race for California (CA-36), was also on the receiving end of horrendous sexism in an online political ad. She too used the Name It. Change It. findings to her advantage, and as a result the attacks completely backfired on her opponent. No matter what office you run for, you and your supporters (or a third party) need to be ready to respond directly to any sexist attacks. If you respond correctly, it might just be the margin that puts you over the top.

The worst thing to have happen to you by the media is to be ignored. If you are being ignored, you are not seen as a credible candidate. Take the time to get to know the political reporters and fair and balanced bloggers. Offer accessibility and treat them like you would a voter or constituent, with respect and honesty and hope they will be fair to you.

### Takeaways

⊃ Negative smears aren't as bad as they might feel at first.

⊃ Personal attacks are merely a distraction.

⊃ Stay focused on your chief objectives—talking to voters/raising money.

⊃ Your coat of armor comes from experience and deflecting smears.

⊃ Be prepared for negative attacks—know what they look like.

⊃ Be on guard when at public events/forums with your opponent.

⊃ Don't email or tweet something you wouldn't want the world to know.

⊃ Assume you are also being recorded or photographed.

⊃ Don't drink alcohol in public or get into a car with anyone who has been drinking.

⊃ Ignore the negative political bloggers, but use them to your advantage when possible.

⊃ When sexist comments are made about you, don't ignore it, call it out.

# 12

# Give Them Something To Talk About

*"If I want to knock a story off the front page,*
*I just change my hairstyle."*

*Hillary Clinton*

Running for office is one time in your life when you want people talking about you. Name recognition is one of the huge hurdles for first-time candidates, and your job is to give the voters a reason to talk about you. When people meet you for the first time, you want them to come away thinking "wow, that is an impressive woman."

Mayor Gale Cherry from Princeton, Kentucky says that women "need to show their strength, be tough and not be intimidated." Mayor

Cherry believes it is important to "accomplish things physically." She hunts, carries a gun, is a member of the National Rifle Association, and she lets people know it. While hunting and guns do not play well in every community, Mayor Cherry knows her people and knew her physical "toughness" would help her overcome any issues about whether a woman would be qualified to serve as mayor.

To be seen as a "wow" candidate, women need to hone their skills as public speakers and make the effort to look the part.

Your appearance as a female candidate will come under such scrutiny. The media will often do their part to perpetuate gender stereotypes that are much harder on women. When Jennifer Lawless ran for Congress in Rhode Island at age 30, she described a scene where a voter replied "Thirty? You don't even look 13. I'm not sure I can support you, but I'd love to hire you as a babysitter."

While it is extremely unfair that women are held to a higher standard, recognize it and accept that while you are trying to become an elected official, you need to look and act the part.

## How to Look and Act the Part

Women candidates need to look professional—suits, blazers, button down blouses, slacks and skirts. Hillary Clinton was teased and made fun of for always wearing her trademark pantsuits, but she always looked as if she belonged on a stage full of men.

Remember Melanie Griffith's famous line in the movie *Working Girl*? "If you want to be taken seriously, you've got to have serious hair." You have to look the part. Enough said about that.

The most important thing for women candidates with regard to shoes is that they are comfortable. You will often be standing and talking to people for three hours at a time at events. A female judicial candidate landed herself in the hospital when a blister on her foot became seriously infected. She lost more than a week on the campaign trail. Put fashion for your feet aside for a few months and go for comfort and support.

## Enthusiasm is Infectious

Voters can tell the difference between a highly enthused candidate and someone whose heart is not fully in the game. People want to be inspired by their leaders and your number one campaign weapon is to show people what you're made of, and what you will do for them when you are elected to office. Show your enthusiasm, sparkle, shine—whatever you want to call it. Just show that you are fired up to get in there and make a difference.

Mayor Kim McMillan of Clarksville, Tennessee stood out among her eight opponents for the mayor's seat in 2010 because she had a depth of experience and was able to communicate to voters that she would be able to hit the ground running if elected. Mayor McMillan served 12 years in the Tennessee legislature and even considered a run for governor before deciding to run for mayor. "When you do something you really love, it shows," says McMillan. "People need to know that as a candidate you are running for the right reasons—to truly make a difference for the community."

**Tell Your Story**

Display confidence and tell a compelling story. Weave a story about your life, and tie the obstacles you've overcome into your campaign message.

Senate candidate Julie Smith-Morrow talked about her tough times as a single mother when her refrigerator was empty, her cabinets were bare and she worried about how she would feed her children. She managed to put herself through school, earn a Ph.D. and become a successful executive. Julie used her humble beginnings to show people that she would never forget the struggles of everyday people and the need to support programs that ensure children are fed, clothed and educated.

Ohio Supreme Court Justice Yvette McGee Brown talked about how difficult it was to afford college, let alone complete law school and pass the bar exam. At age 27 she oversaw 900 cases working for the Ohio Department of Corrections. Seeing children locked up made an impact that moved her focus towards child advocacy and protection. At age 32 McGee Brown was encouraged to run for judge and won her first election by defeating a sitting judge. As a candidate, her story was very compelling and a perfect match for her race.

"Women need to be prepared to tell their story, to be in control of their story and be comfortable in telling it," says Chris Jahnke, speech consultant and author of *The Well Spoken Woman*. "Likability is so much more important than it used to be and is just as important as being able to demonstrate your toughness."

"Candidates need to be able to talk about their family, hobbies, interests, what have they have done to improve their community," added Jahnke.

## Your Image/Brand

Everyone has their own personal style. Voters will respond to you, and have an easier time connecting and talking about you, if you display a consistent image. Based on your personality, campaign message, stump speeches, personal contacts with hundreds or thousands of people, you will develop an image that becomes your brand.

Will you be known as a fighter? Compromiser? Trusted leader? Businesslike taxpayer watchdog? Make a decision about the image you want to convey, then make sure that everything you say, do and that comes from your campaign reinforces that image.

---

*Make a decision about the image you want to convey, then make sure that everything reinforces that image.*

---

Barack Obama's campaign for president established a strong brand that was centered around a single theme of hope. His graphics, image and his brand all reflected that feeling of freshness and hope.

From the graphic look, to the fonts, and even to the colors used, all these elements should reflect your theme, your image and message. Every piece of communication should reflect your brand; signs, website, email communications, hand-outs, badges and stickers. Most importantly, be consistent.

**Now Go Run**

Skilled politicians are admired because they seem to have that special gift. Some call it charisma, but more likely it is a combination of talent, skill, preparation, perseverance, and resiliency. You can develop the skills you need to show voters that you have the talent to be an effective candidate and ultimately an elected official.

Develop your best self. Seek all the help and training you can, and build the confidence you will need. Good candidates do not happen by accident—they are developed and encouraged. Honor the calling of public service. Now I'm encouraging you.

Now go run!

*"It is what we make of what we have, not what we are given, that separates one person from another."*
*Nelson Mandela*

*Pink Politics*

# Part IV

## Resources

# Books

Feldt, Gloria (2010) *No Excuses—9 Ways Women Can Change How We Think About Power*, New York, Avalon Publishing Group

Lawless, Jennifer L. *Becoming A Candidate: Political Ambition and the Decision to Run for Office*, New York: Cambridge University Press, forthcoming.

Lawless, Jennifer L. and Richard L. Fox. (2010) *It Still Takes A Candidate: Why Women Don't Run for Office*, New York: Cambridge University Press.

Lawless, Jennifer L. and Richard L. Fox. (2005) *It Takes A Candidate: Why Women Don't Run for Office*, New York: Cambridge University Press.

Kunin, Madeleine M.(2008) *Pearls Politics & Power: How Women Can Win and Lead*, Vermont: Chelsea Green Publishing Company.

Jahnke, Chris (2011) *The Well Spoken Woman*, Washington D.C., Prometheus Books.

Lee, Barbara (2001) *Keys to the Governor's Office and Governor Guidebook series*, Boston, Barbara Lee Family Foundation

Wilson, Marie (2004) *Closing the Leadership Gap - Why Women Can and Must Help Run the World*, New York, Penguin Books

# Organization Websites

Barbara Lee Family Foundation
*www.barbaraleefoundation.org*

Center for American Women & Politics
*www.cawp.rutgers.edu*

ElectWomen
*www.electwomen.com*

Emerge America
*www.emergeamerica.org*

EMILY's List
*www.emilyslist.org*

Institute for Women's Policy Research
*www.iwpr.org*

League of Women Voters
*www.lwv.org*

Name It. Change It.
*www.nameitchangeit.org*

National Foundation for Women Legislators
*www.womenlegislators.org*

National Council of Women's Organizations
*www.womensorganizations.org*

National Organization for Women
*www.now.org*

National Women's Political Caucus
*www.nwpc.org*

Off the Sidelines
*www.offthesidelines.org*

Progressive Majority
*www.progressivemajority.org*

Running Start
*www.runningstartonline.org*

She Should Run
*www.sheshouldrun.org*

The Feminist Majority
*www.feminist.org*

The White House Project
*www.thewhitehouseproject.org*

Women's Media Center
*www.womensmediacenter.com*

Women and Politics Institute
*www.american.edu/spa/wpi*

Women Count
*www.womencount.org*

Women's Campaign Fund
*www.wcfonline.org*

WUFPAC-Women Under Forty Political Action Committee
*www.wufpac.org*

# Candidate Resources

American Association of Political Consultants
*www.theaapc.org*

BlogHer Women's Political Blog
*www.blogher.com/member/sarah-granger*

Campaigns & Elections Magazine
*www.campaignsandelections.com*

ElectWomen
*www.electwomen.com*

Federal Election Commission
*www.fec.gov*

Open Secrets Center for Responsive Politics
*www.opensecrets.org/elections*

Project Vote Smart
*www.votesmart.org*

# About The Author

Kathy Groob is the founder of *ElectWomen*, dedicated to helping elect women to public office. *ElectWomen.com* is a comprehensive website offering women a place to read about other women running for public office and connect with a wealth of campaign resources, books, training opportunities, and workshops. Kathy has assembled a distinguished panel of contributors who provide articles and responses to reader questions.

Kathy is a 30-year+ businesswoman and entrepreneur and has served as an elected city official and ran for the Kentucky Senate in 2008. She has been a mentor and advocate for women in the workplace throughout her career. Her Senate campaign inspired hundreds of women to become involved and she created a bipartisan network of campaign volunteers and supporters. She is a political consultant and co-owner of *November Strategies,* a co-founder of *Emerge Kentucky,* and a leader in many women's organizations.

Kathy resides in Kentucky with her husband Jeff and has three adult children. Outside of politics, Kathy is involved with efforts to provide support to the homeless and people living in poverty in her community.

To request a speaking engagement or for information about additional training and campaign services contact Kathy Groob at www.ElectWomen.com or at 859-291-9001.

Made in the USA
Charleston, SC
09 September 2013